Copyright © 2021 by Happy Lion

ISBN: 9798732067316

First paperback edition April 2021

Tracing lines and curves

Improve your pen control

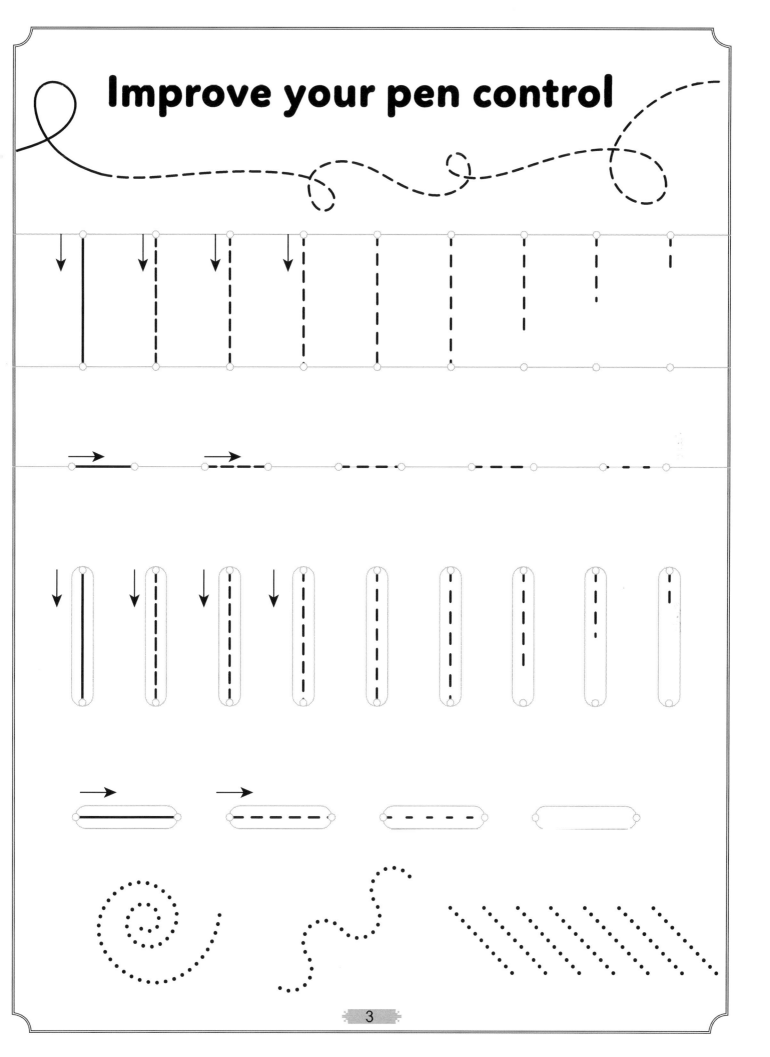

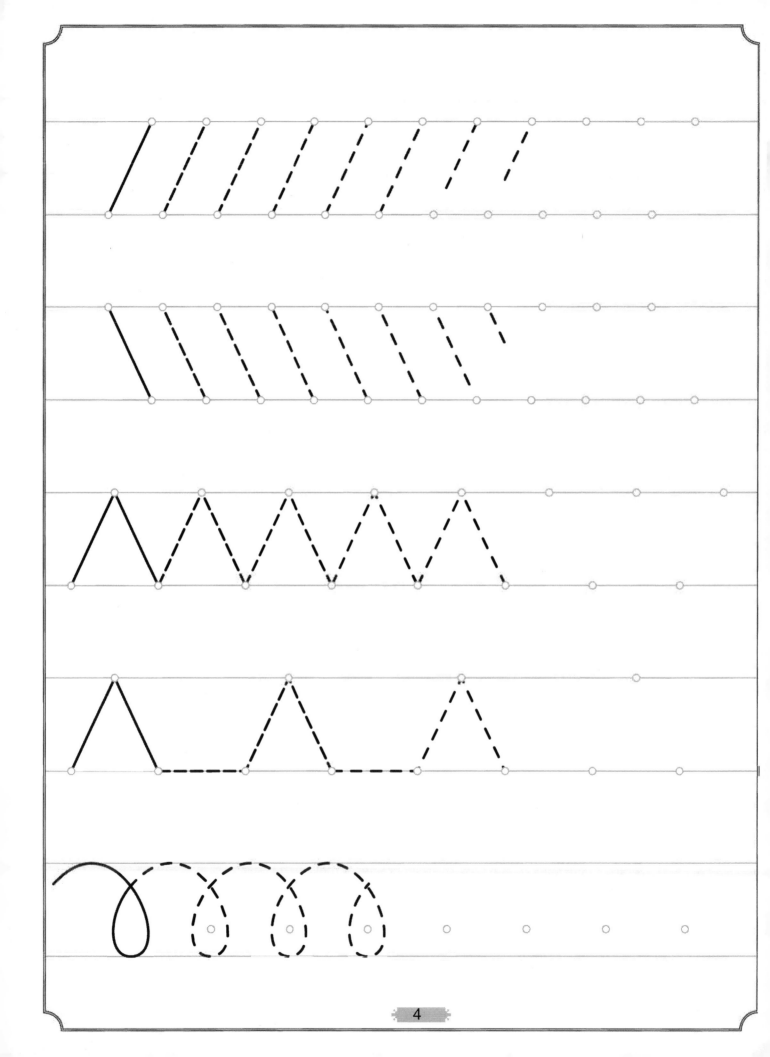

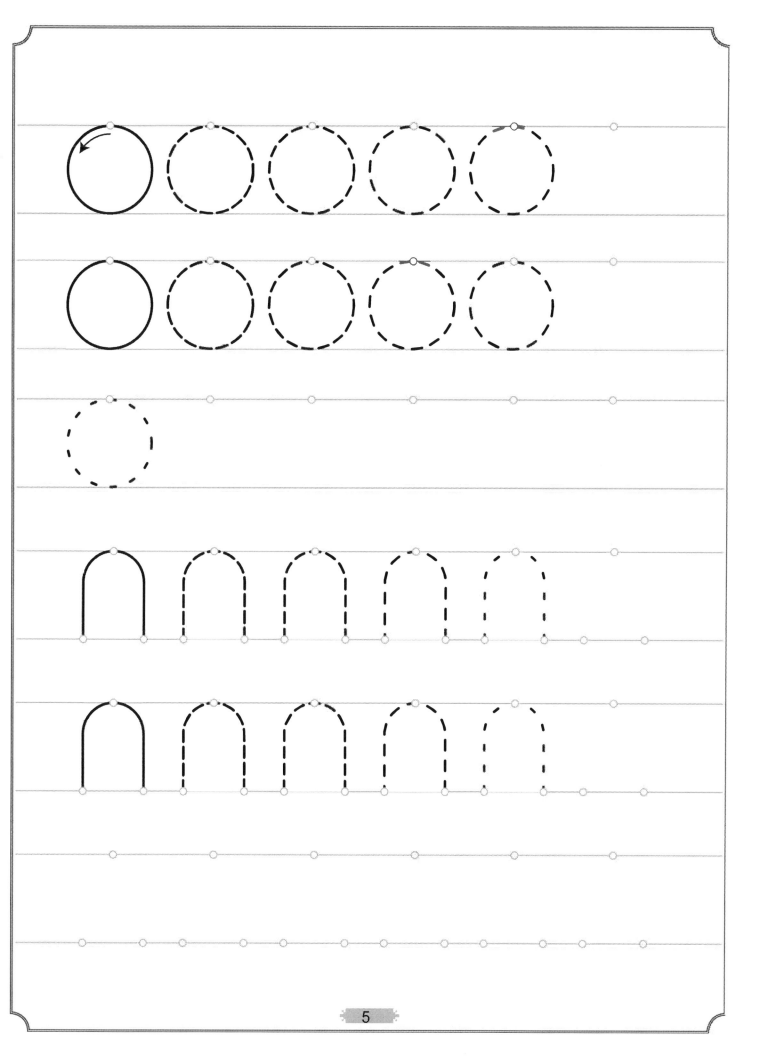

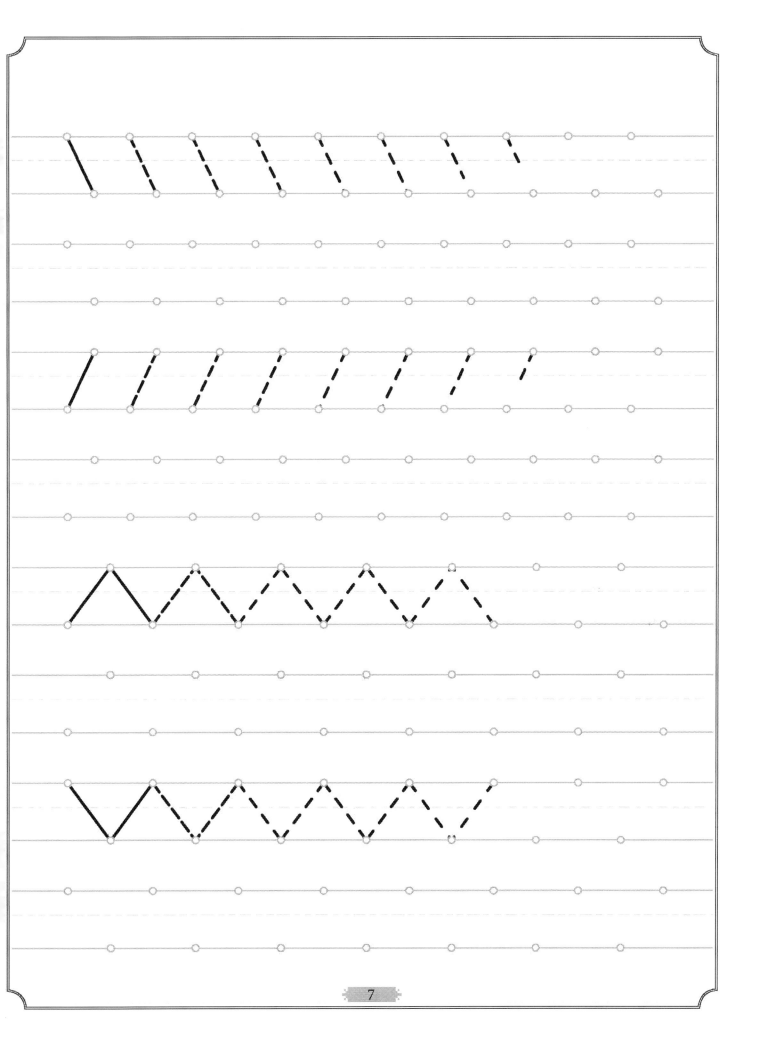

Let's learn and trace the alphabet

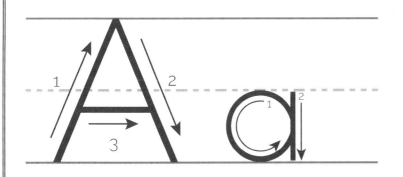

Trace the letters.

Apple

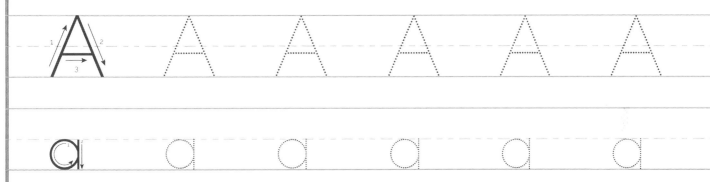

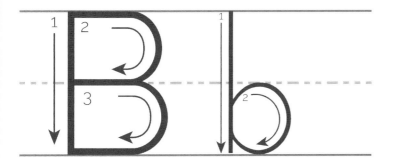

Trace the letters.

Ball

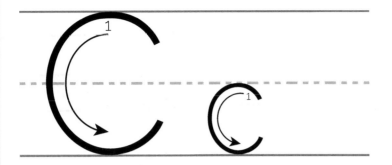

Cat

Trace the letters.

   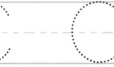

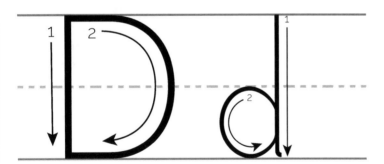

Dog

Trace the letters.

E e

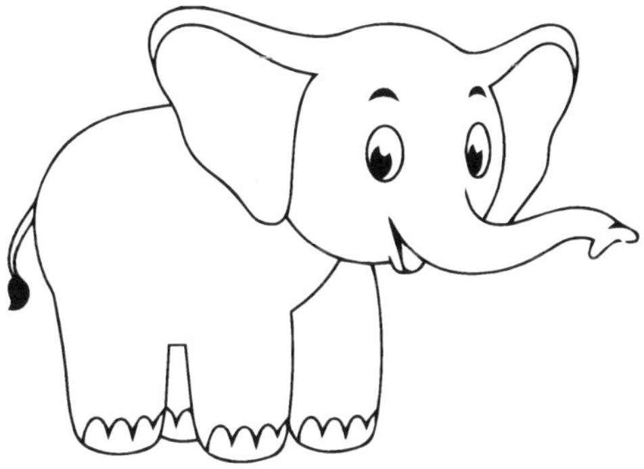

Trace the letters.

Elephant

E E E E E E

e e e e e e

F f

Trace the letters.

Fish

F F F F F F

f f f f f f

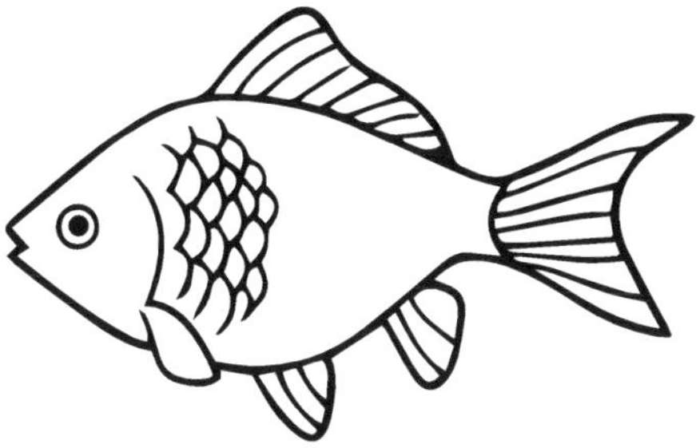

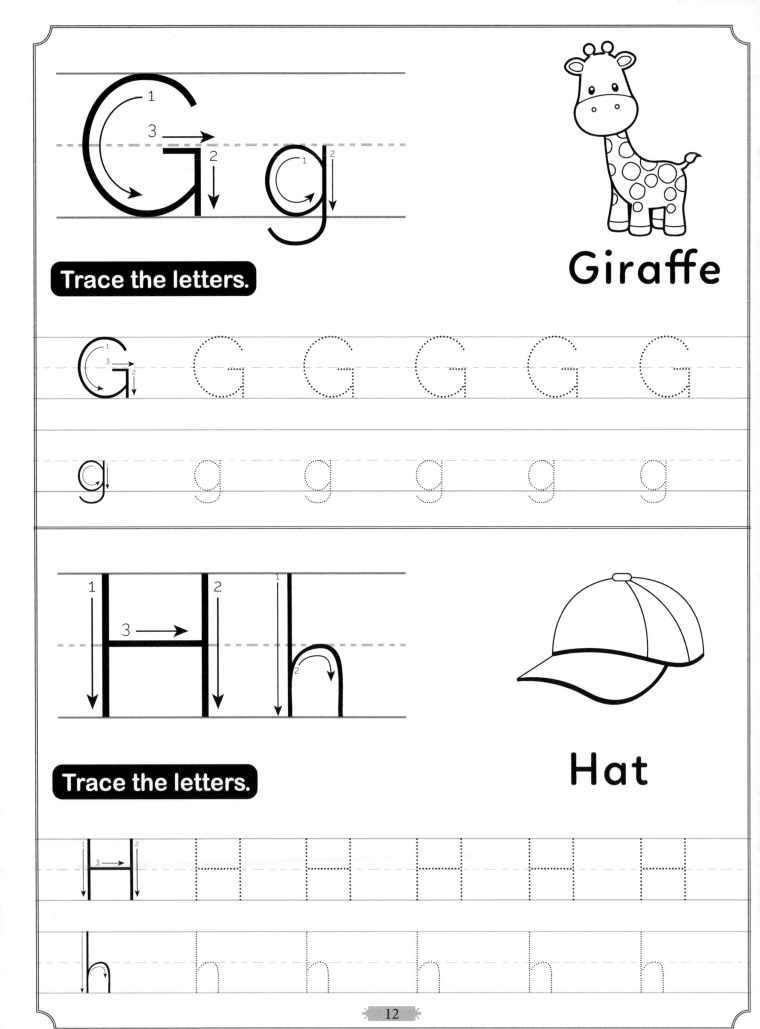

Trace the letters.

Giraffe

Trace the letters.

Hat

12

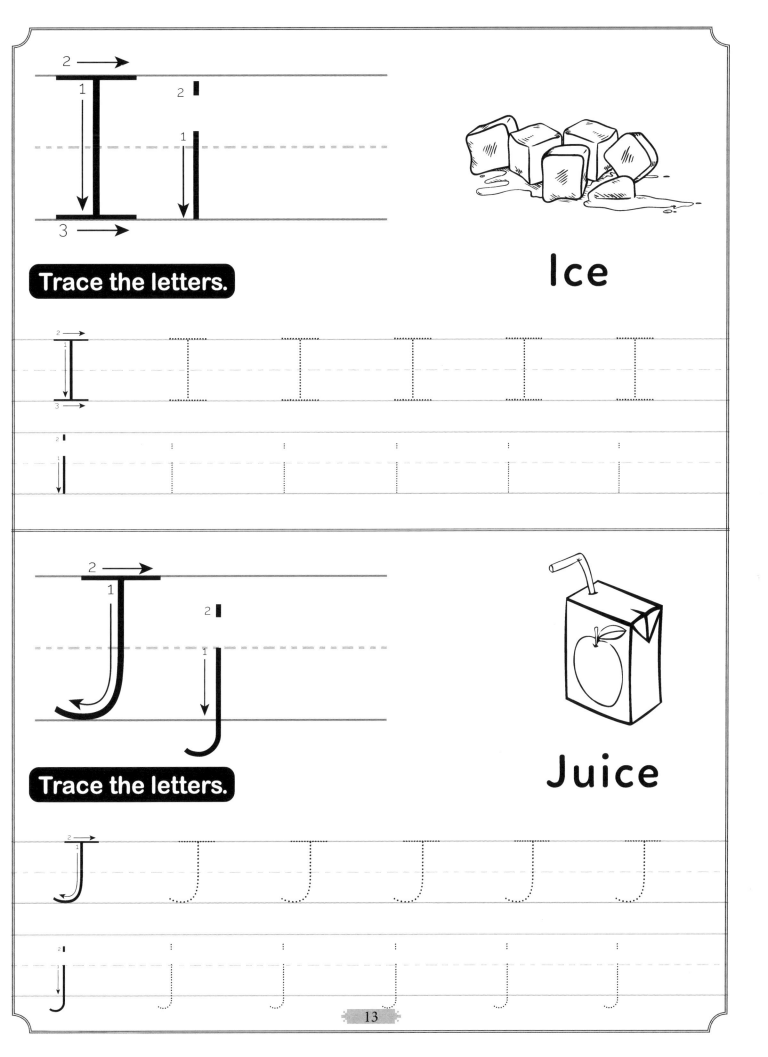

Trace the letters.

Ice

Trace the letters.

Juice

13

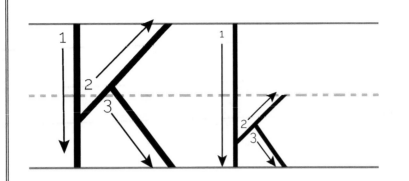

Kangaroo

Trace the letters.

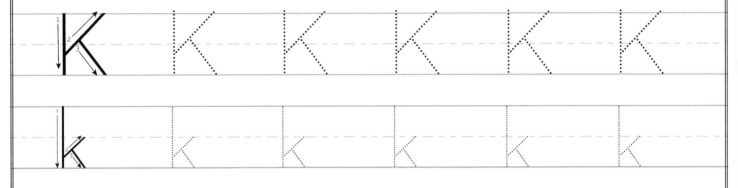

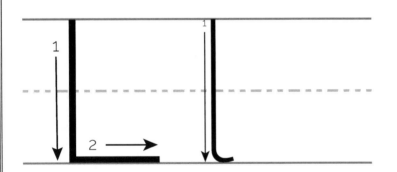

Lion

Trace the letters.

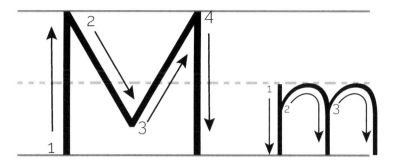

Trace the letters.

Mango

M M M M M M M

m m m m m m m

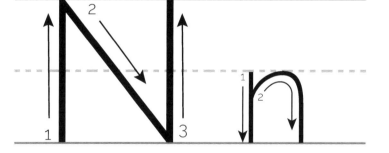

Trace the letters.

Nest

N N N N N N N

n n n n n n n

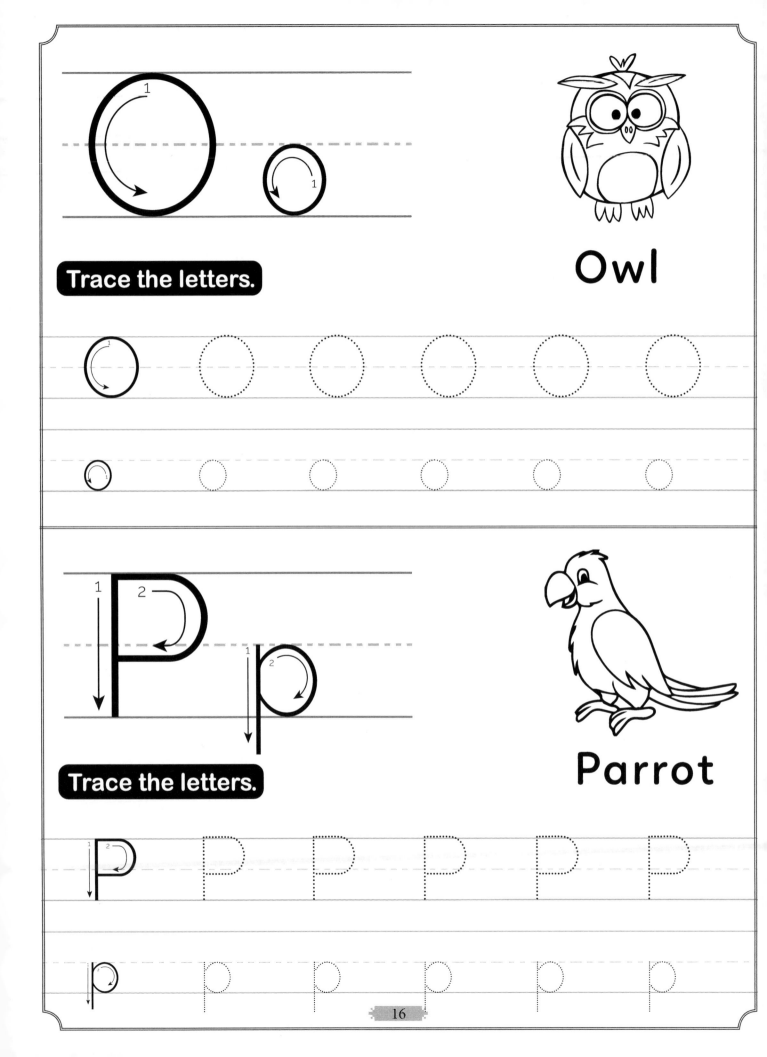

Trace the letters.

Owl

Trace the letters.

Parrot

16

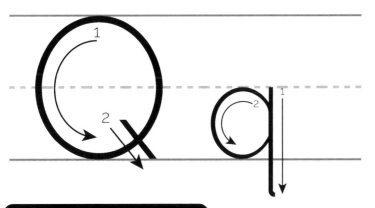

Queen

Trace the letters.

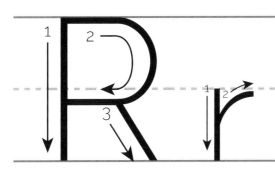

Rabbit

Trace the letters.

R   R   R   R   R   R

r   r   r   r   r   r

Sun

Trace the letters.

S S S S S S S

s s s s s s s

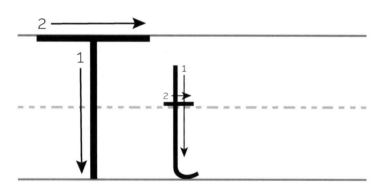

Turtle

Trace the letters.

 T T T T T

t t t t t t

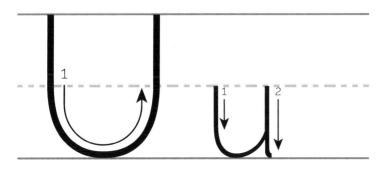

Trace the letters.

Umbrella

U U U U U U U

u u u u u u

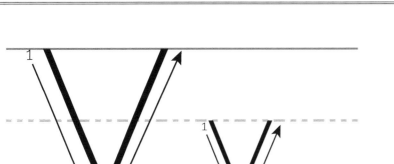

Trace the letters.

Van

V V V V V V V

v v v v v v v

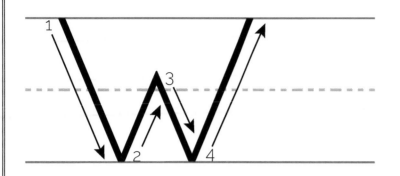

Trace the letters.

Watch

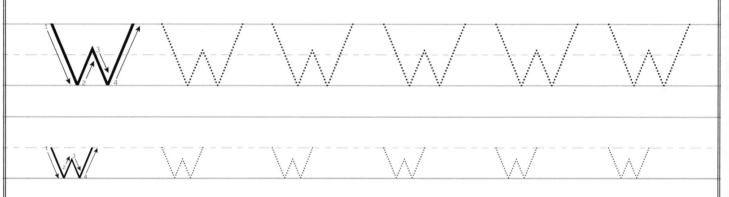

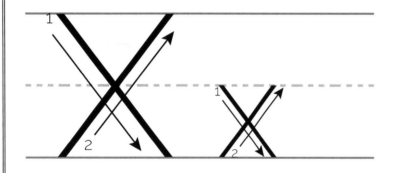

Trace the letters.

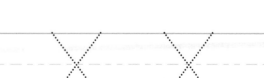

Xylophone

Y y

Trace the letters.

Yak

Y Y Y Y Y Y

y y y y y y

Z z

Trace the letters.

Zebra

Z Z Z Z Z Z

z z z z z z

Let's learn and trace the numbers

1

One

1 1 1 1 1 1 1

1 1 1 1 1 1 1

1 1 1 1 1 1 1

One One One

One One One

One One One

2

Two

2 2 2 2 2 2 2 2 2 2

2 2 2 2 2 2 2 2 2 2

2 2 2 2 2 2 2 2 2 2

Two Two Two

Two Two Two

Two Two Two

3

Three

3 3 3 3 3 3 3 3 3

3 3 3 3 3 3 3 3

3 3 3 3 3 3 3 3

Three Three Three

Three Three Three

Three Three Three

4
Four

4 4 4 4 4 4 4 4 4

4 4 4 4 4 4 4 4 4

4 4 4 4 4 4 4 4 4

Four Four Four

Four Four Four

Four Four Four

5

Five

5 5 5 5 5 5 5 5

5 5 5 5 5 5 5 5

5 5 5 5 5 5 5 5

Five Five Five

Five Five Five

Five Five Five

6

Six

6 6 6 6 6 6 6 6 6

6 6 6 6 6 6 6 6 6

6 6 6 6 6 6 6 6 6

Six   Six   Six

Six   Six   Six

Six   Six   Six

7

Seven

7 7 7 7 7 7 7 7 7 7 7
7 7 7 7 7 7 7 7 7 7 7
7 7 7 7 7 7 7 7 7 7 7

Seven Seven Seven
Seven Seven Seven
Seven Seven Seven

8

Eight

8

8 8 8 8 8 8 8

8 8 8 8 8 8 8

8 8 8 8 8 8 8

Eight   Eight   Eight

Eight   Eight   Eight

Eight   Eight   Eight

9

Nine

9 9 9 9 9 9 9 9

9 9 9 9 9 9 9 9

9 9 9 9 9 9 9 9

Nine Nine Nine

Nine Nine Nine

Nine Nine Nine

10

Ten

10 10 10 10 10 10 10

10 10 10 10 10 10 10

10 10 10 10 10 10 10

Ten   Ten   Ten

Ten   Ten   Ten

Ten   Ten   Ten

11 Eleven

11 11 11 11 11 11 11 11

11 11 11 11 11 11 11

Eleven   Eleven

The mouse can not find cheese. Will you show him the way?

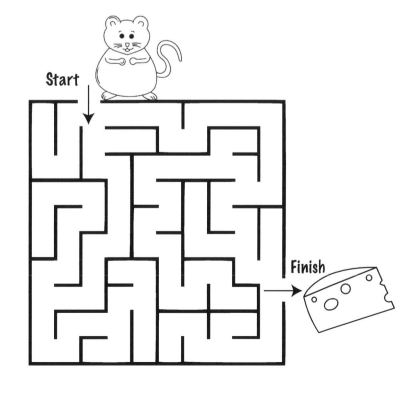

Start

Finish

12 Twelve

Connect the dots and color it.

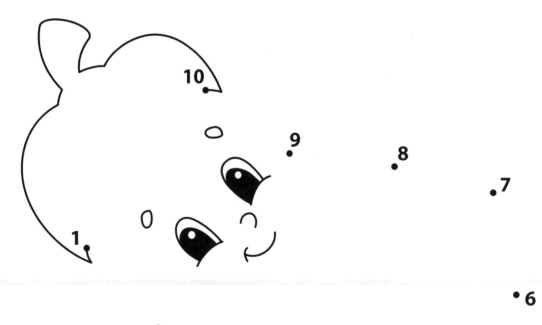

13 Thirteen

13 13 13 13 13 13 13 13

13 13 13 13 13 13 13 13

Thirteen Thirteen

Connect the images that have something in common.

35

14   Fourteen

14 14 14 14 14 14 14

14 14 14 14 14 14 14

Fourteen   Fourteen

Copy the figure in the side box.

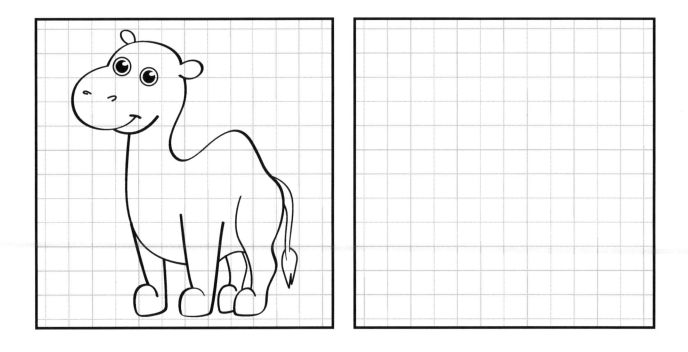

15 Fifteen

15 15 15 15 15 15 15 15

15 15 15 15 15 15 15 15

Fifteen   Fifteen

Connect the images that have something in common.

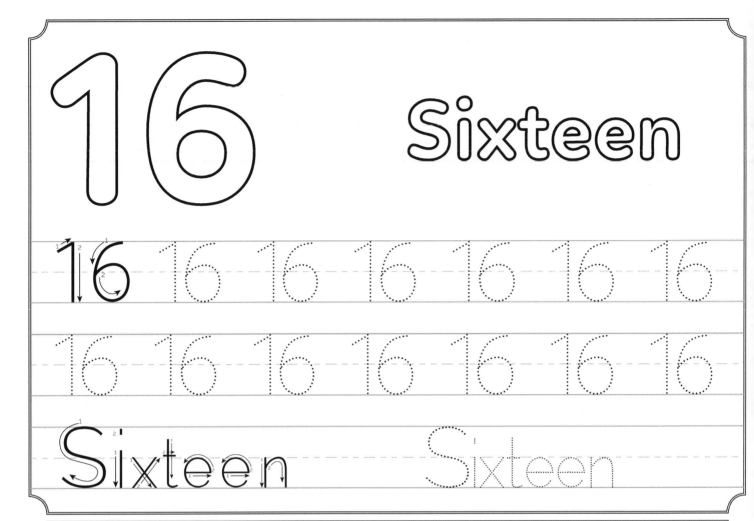

Draw a circle around each letter in the "hat".

17

Seventeen

17 17 17 17 17 17 17 17

17 17 17 17 17 17 17 17

Seventeen Seventeen

Draw yours.

18

Eighteen

18 18 18 18 18 18 18

18 18 18 18 18 18 18

Eighteen   Eighteen

Connect the images that have something in common.

19 Nineteen

19 19 19 19 19 19 19 19

19 19 19 19 19 19 19 19

Nineteen Nineteen

Circle the tallest giraffe.

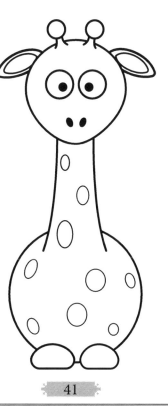

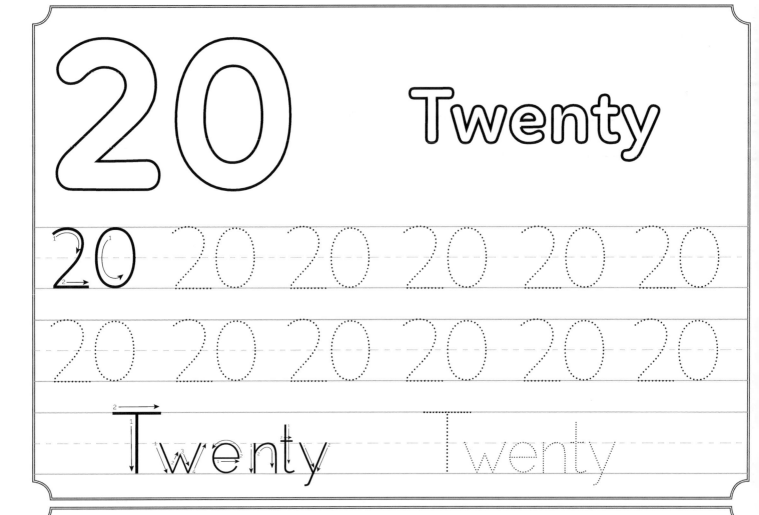

20 Twenty

Choose the correct option to complete the dinosaur.

A

B

C

D

21 Twenty one

Copy the figure in the side box.

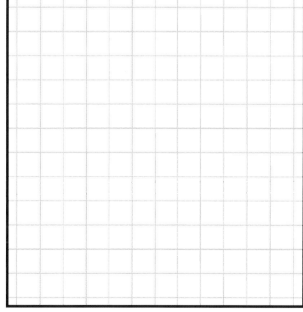

22 Twenty two

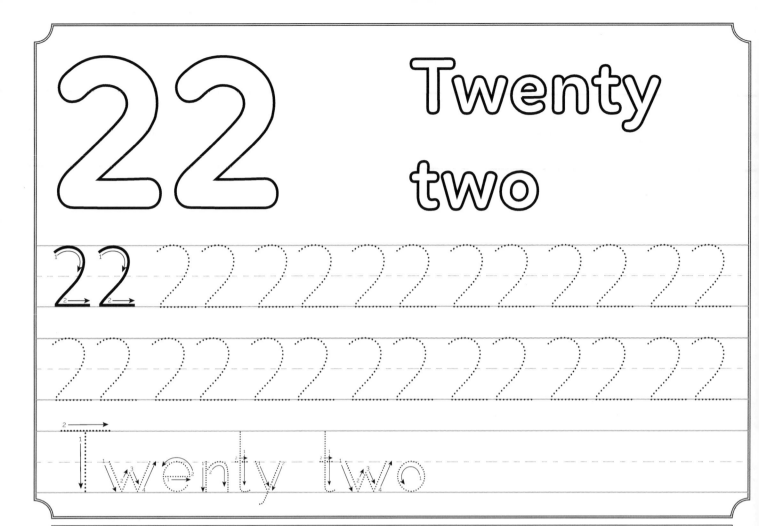

Tiger can not find his baby. Will you show him the way?

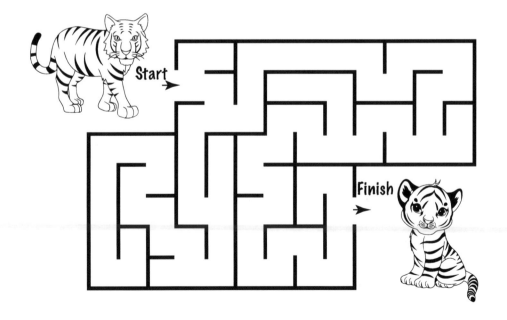

Start

Finish

23

Twenty three

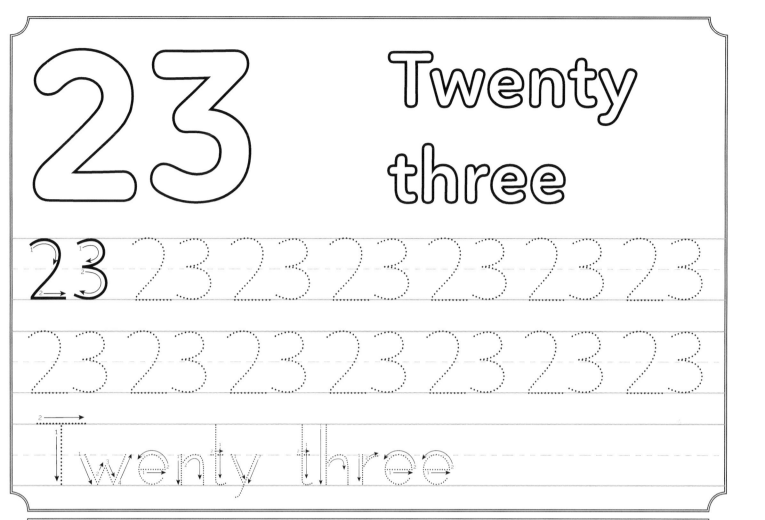

Trace the image and color it!

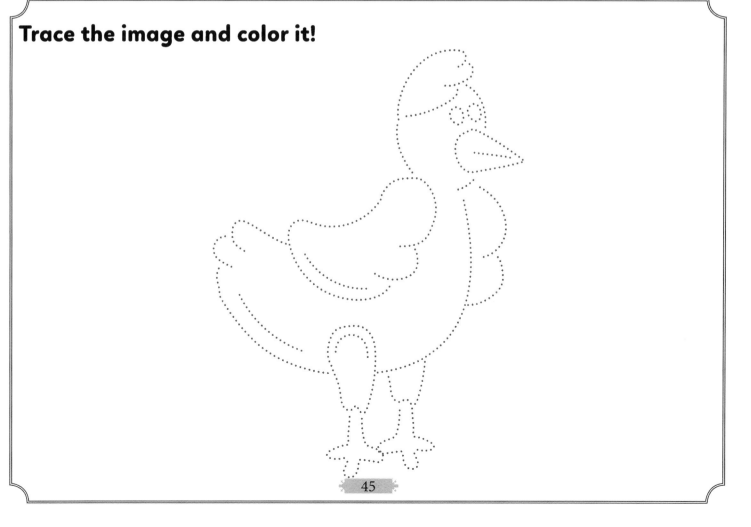

24 Twenty Four

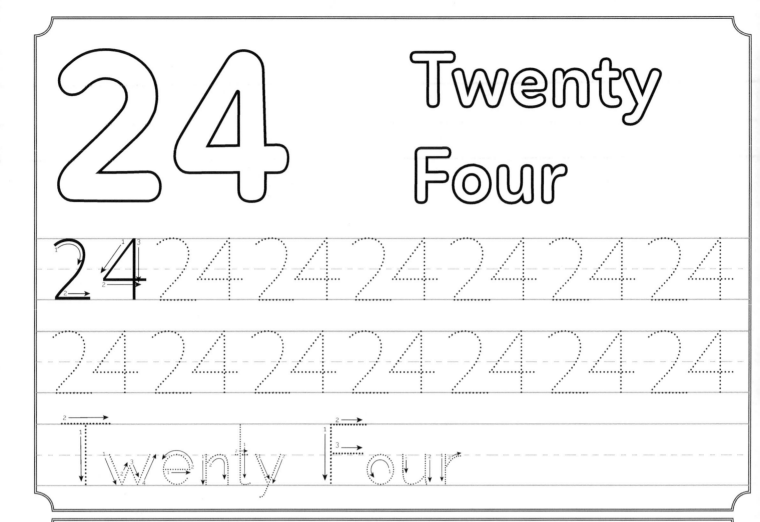

Lion can not find the goat. Will you show him the way?

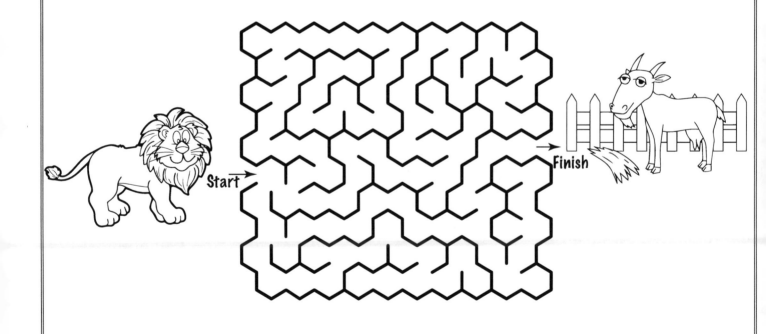

Start

Finish

25

Twenty Five

Connect the images that have something in common.

26 Twenty Six

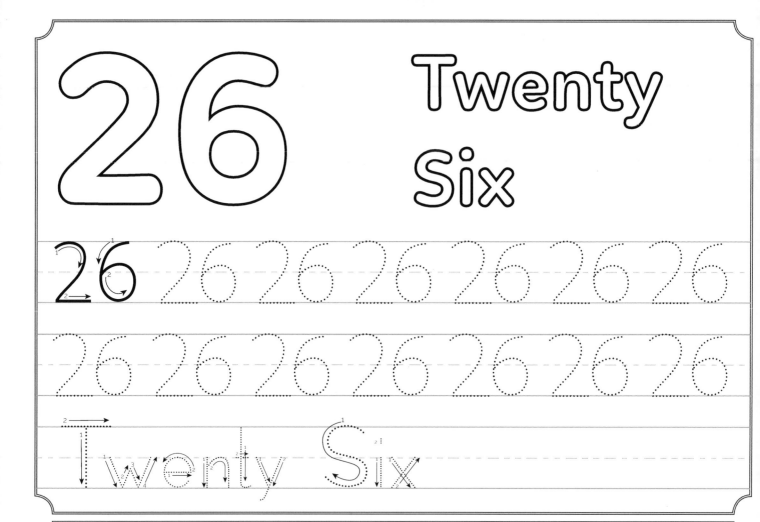

26 26 26 26 26 26 26 26

26 26 26 26 26 26 26 26

Twenty Six

Write the time given on the clock.

27 Twenty Seven

Circle the longest pencil.

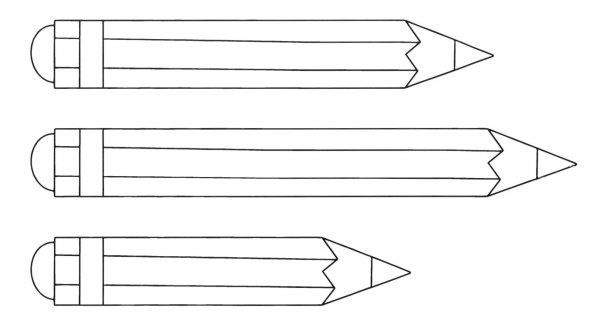

28 Twenty Eight

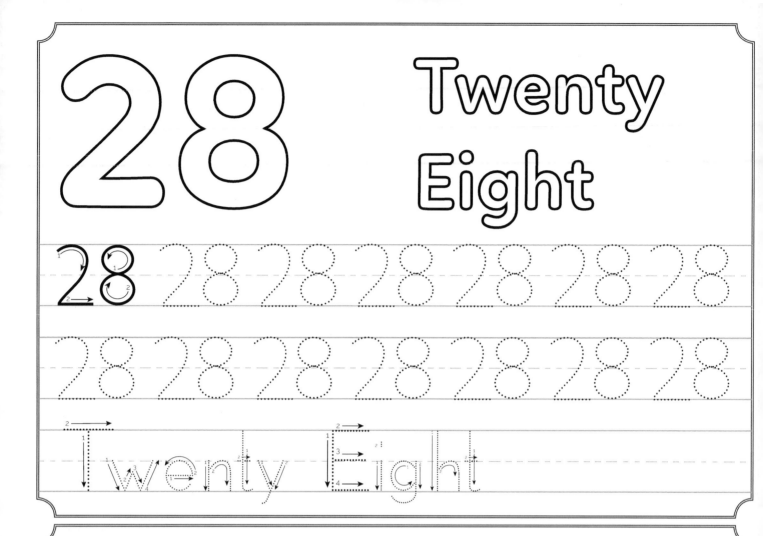

Copy the figure in the side box.

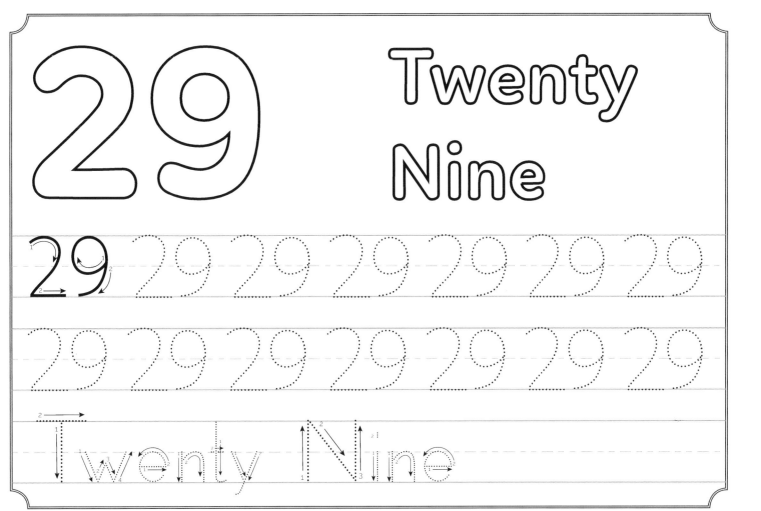

29 Twenty Nine

Draw a circle around each letter in the "pig".

30 Thirty

Connect uppercase and lowercase letters.

Y   o

O   y

V   n

N   v

31

Thirty One

31 31 31 31 31 31 31 31

31 31 31 31 31 31 31

Thirty One

Choose the correct option to complete the dog.

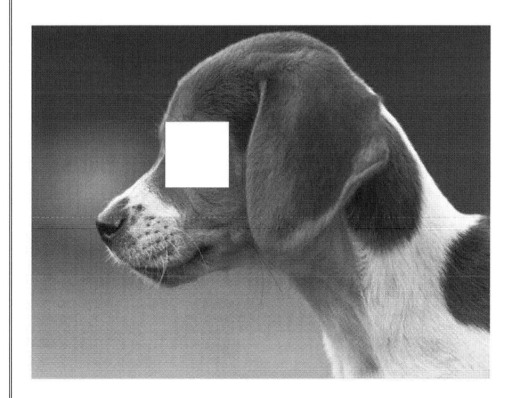

A

B

C

D

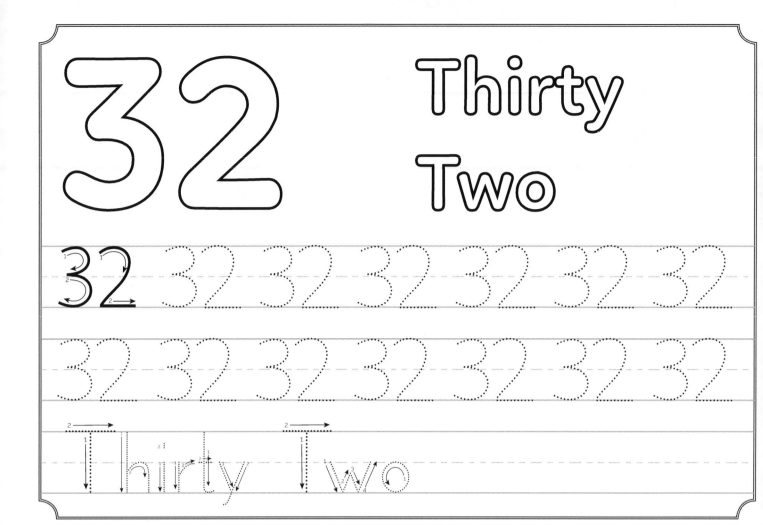

32

Thirty Two

Thirty Two

Sheep can not find his baby. Will you show him the way?

Finish

Start

33

Thirty Three

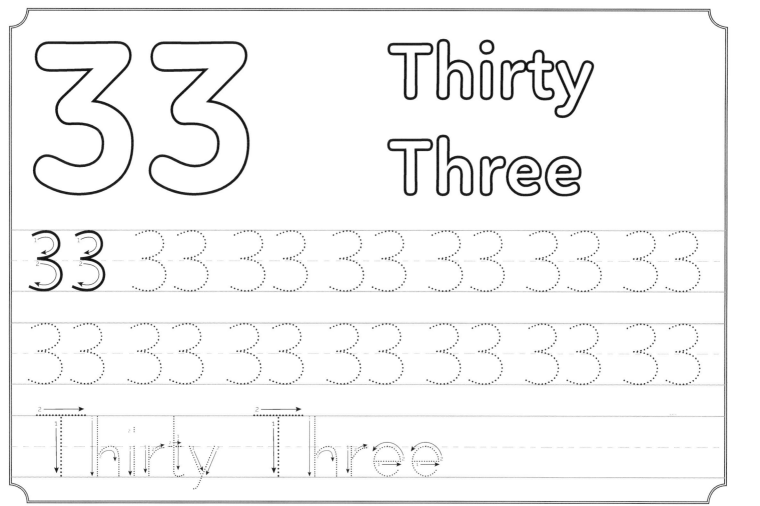

Thirty Three

Connect the images that have something in common

34 Thirty Four

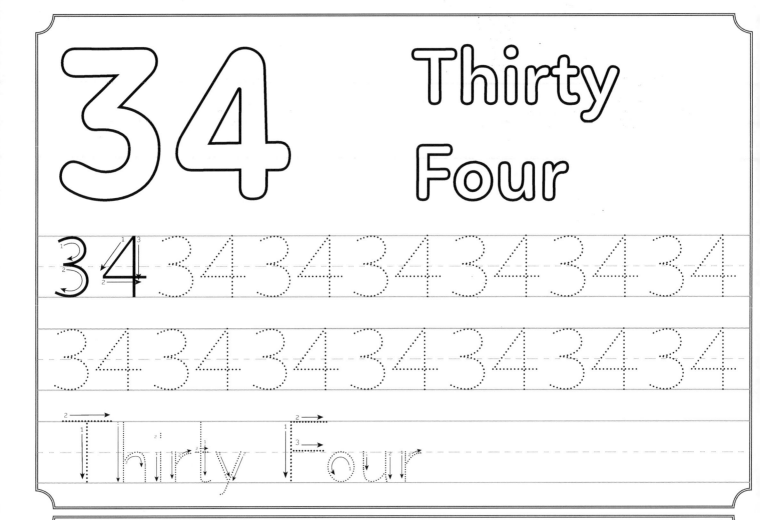

3 4 34 34 34 34 34 34 34

34 34 34 34 34 34 34

Thirty Four

Write the time given on the clock.

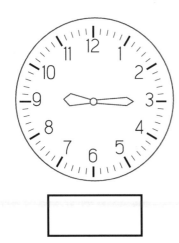

35

Thirty Five

3 5

35 35 35 35 35 35 35 35

35 35 35 35 35 35 35 35

Thirty Five

Connect the images that have something in common

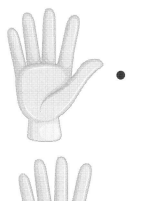 •   •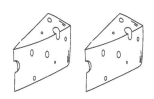

 •   •

 •   •

36 Thirty Six

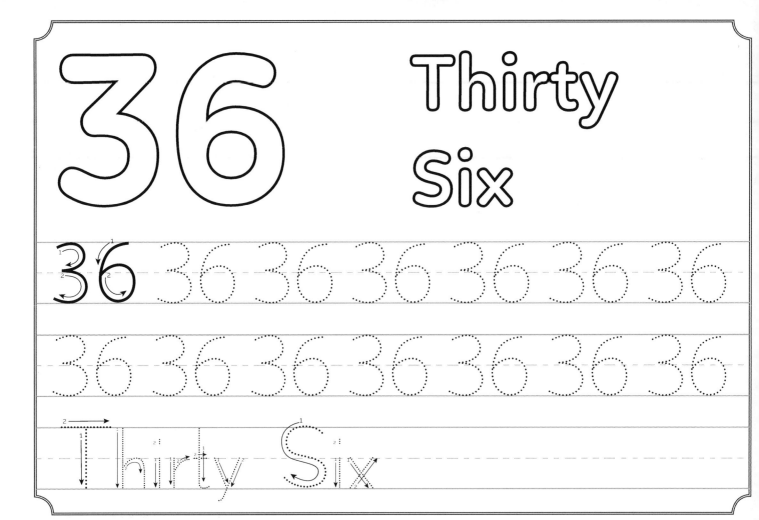

Trace the image and color it!

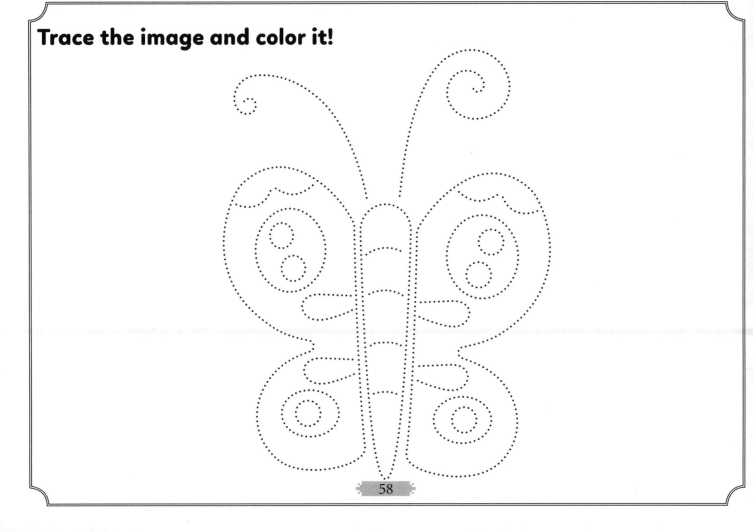

37 Thirty Seven

Connect the dots and color it.

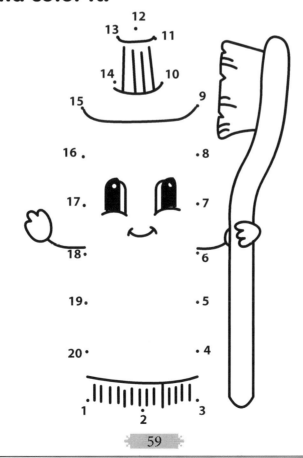

38

Thirty Eight

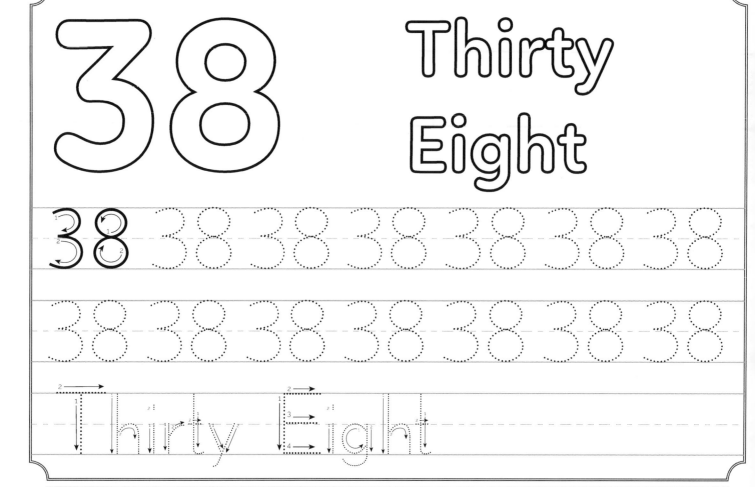

38 38 38 38 38 38 38

38 38 38 38 38 38 38

Thirty Eight

Choose the correct option to complete the butterfly.

A

B

C

D

39

Thirty Nine

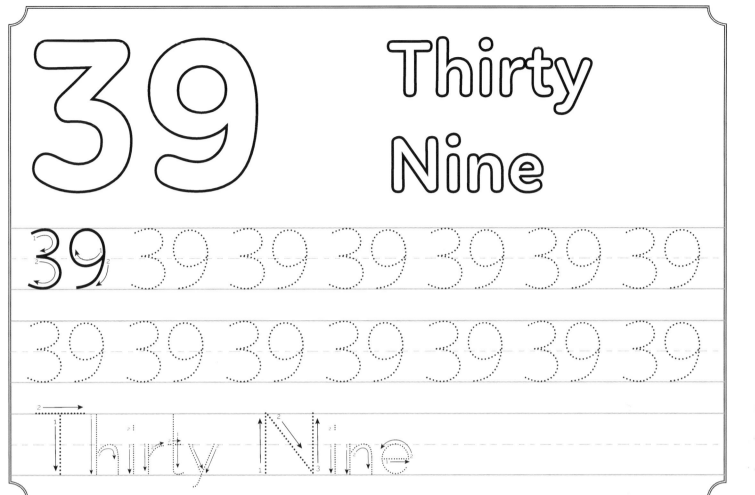

39 39 39 39 39 39 39 39 39

39 39 39 39 39 39 39 39 39

Thirty Nine

Color the frog.

40 Forty

Draw a circle around each letter in the "star".

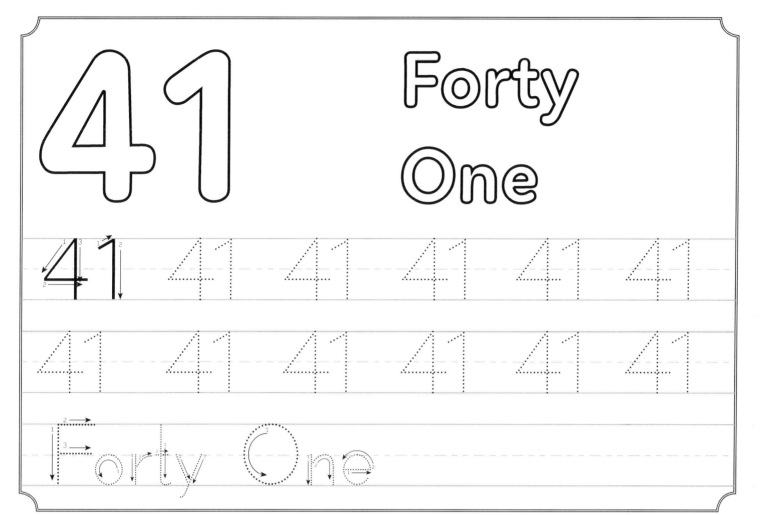

Write the right number and his name.

					5	Five
○	○	○	○	○		
⬡	⬡	⬡	⬡			
▢	▢	▢				

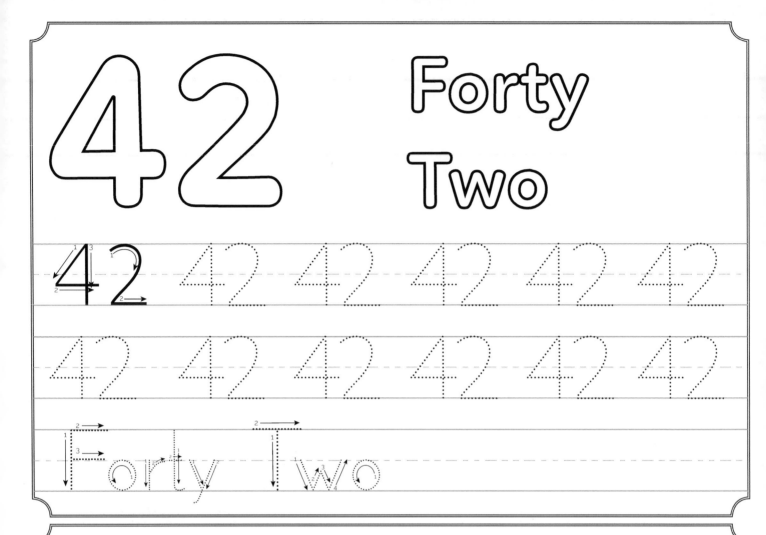

42 Forty Two

Connect the dots and color it.

43

Forty Three

Connect the dots and color it.

44 Forty Four

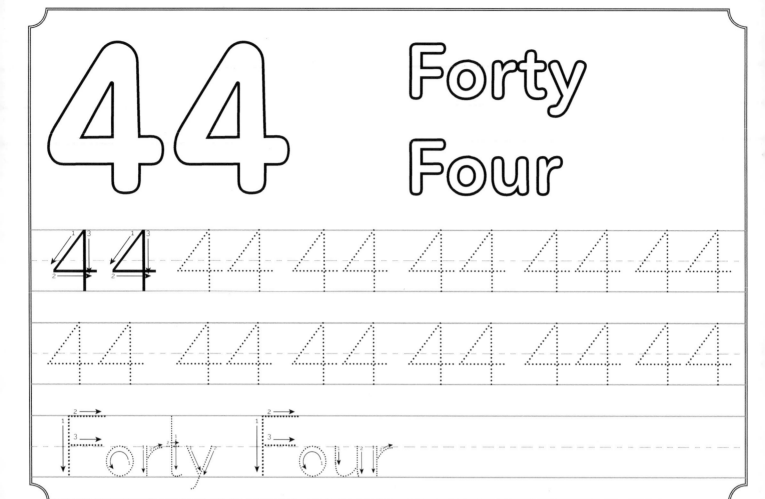

Draw yours.

45

Forty Five

45 45 45 45 45 45 45

45 45 45 45 45 45 45

Forty Five

Ostrich can not find his eggs. Will you show him the way?

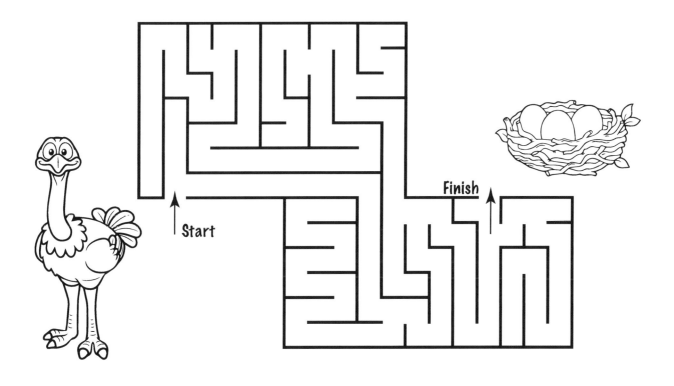

Start

Finish

46

Forty Six

46 46 46 46 46 46

46 46 46 46 46 46

Forty Six

Choose the correct option to complete the camel.

A

B

C

D

47

Forty Seven

47 47 47 47 47 47

47 47 47 47 47 47

Forty Seven

Connect uppercase and lowercase letters.

M   q

B   w

W   b

Q   m

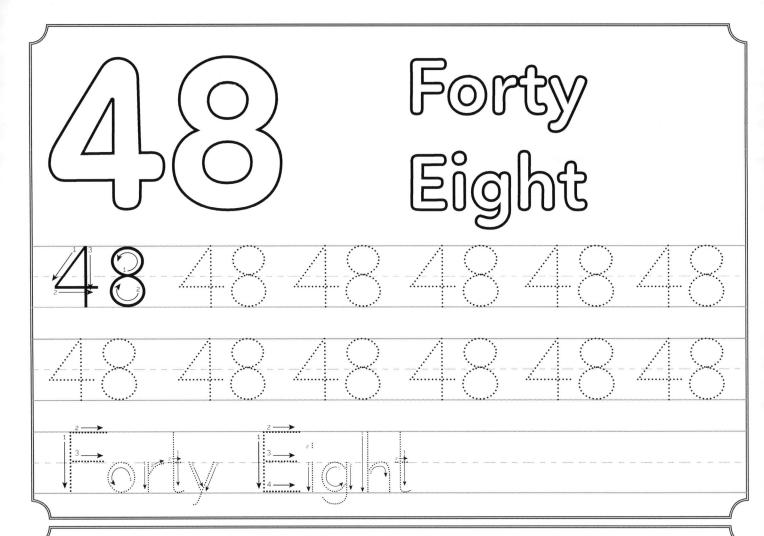

48

Forty
Eight

48 48 48 48 48 48 48 48 48 48 48

Forty Eight

Copy the figure in the side box.

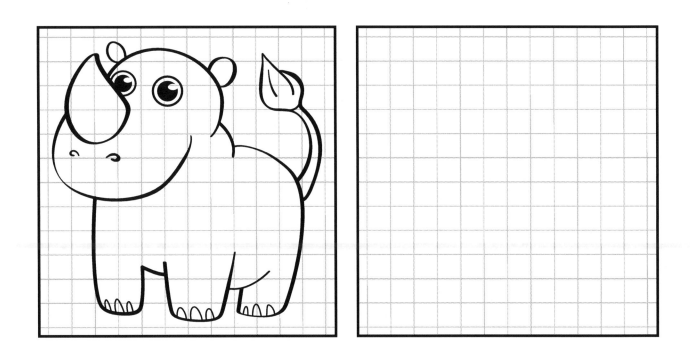

49

Forty Nine

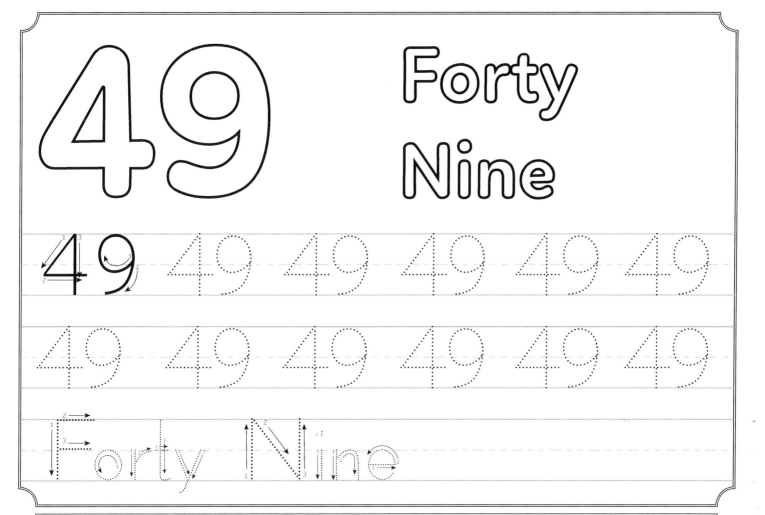

49 49 49 49 49 49

49 49 49 49 49 49

Forty Nine

Trace the image and color it!

50 Fifty

Connect the dots and color it.

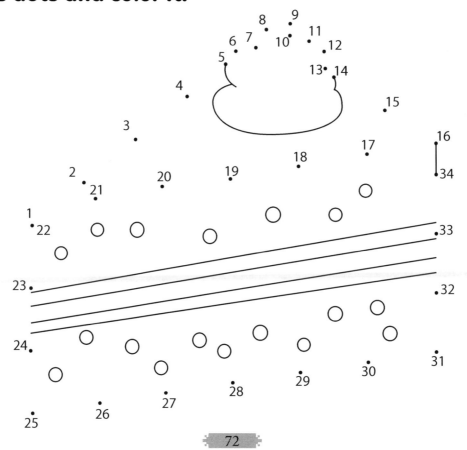

51

Fifty One

5 5 5 5 5 5 5 5 5 5

51 51 51 51 51

Fifty One

Tiger can not find the rabbit. Will you show him the way?

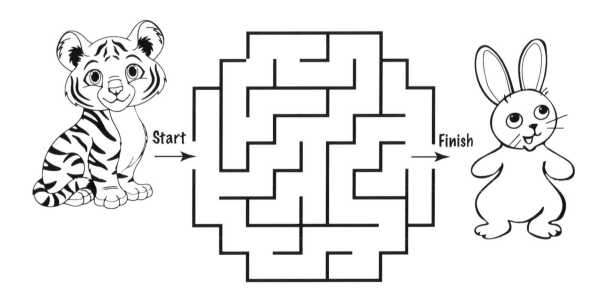

Start   Finish

52 Fifty Two

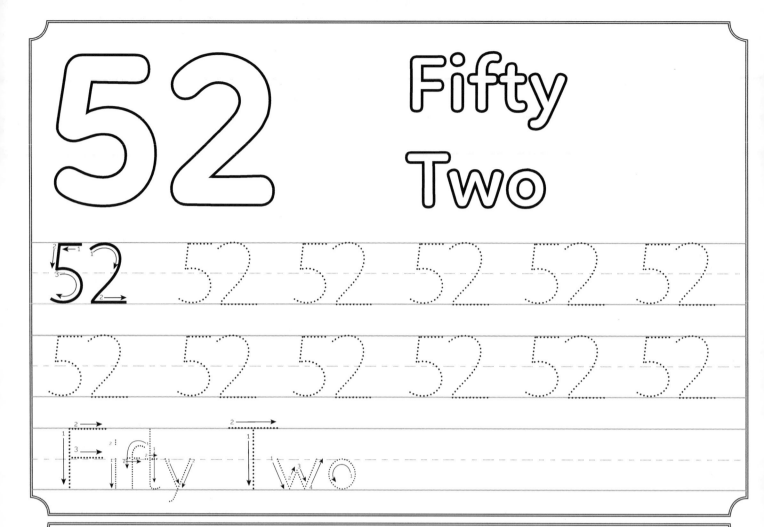

Connect uppercase and lowercase letters.

G   k

T   g

D   d

K   t

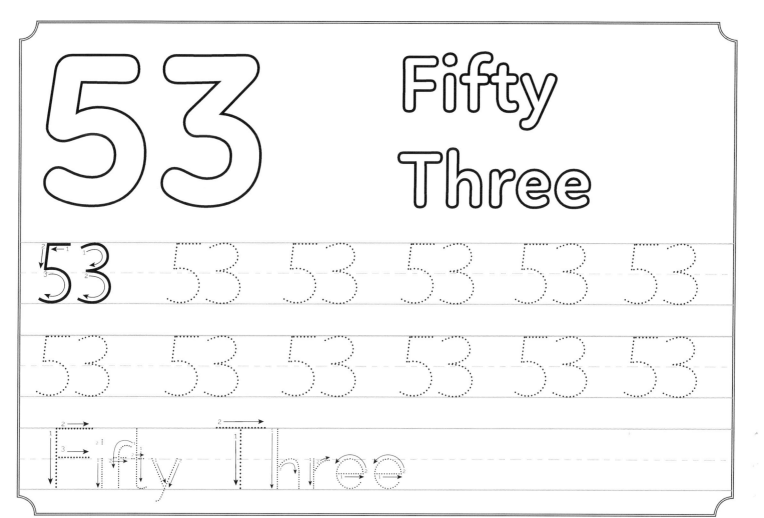

Dolphin can not find his baby. Will you show him the way?

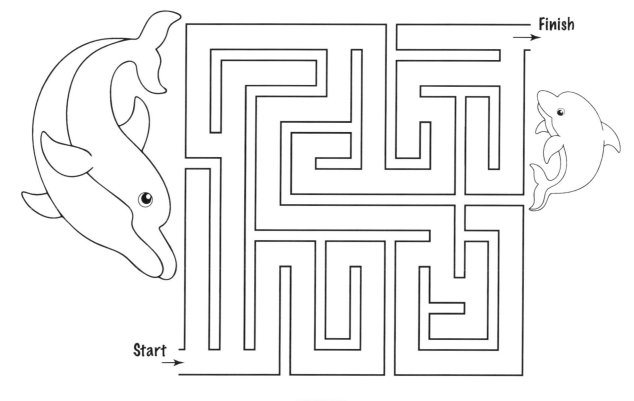

54 Fifty Four

54 54 54 54 54 54

54 54 54 54 54 54

Fifty Four

Draw yours.

55

Fifty Five

Choose the correct option to complete the lion.

A

B

C

D

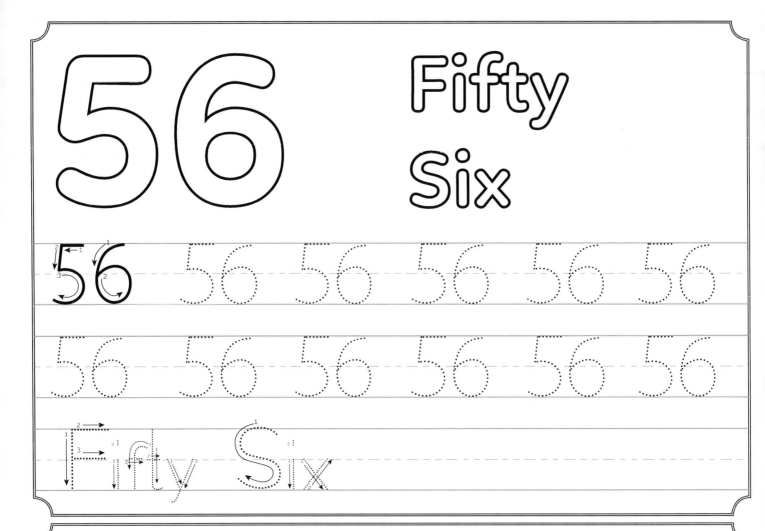

56 Fifty Six

Connect the dots and color it.

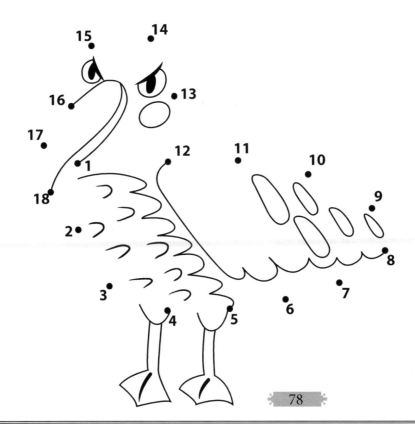

57

Fifty Seven

Copy the figure in the side box.

58

Fifty Eight

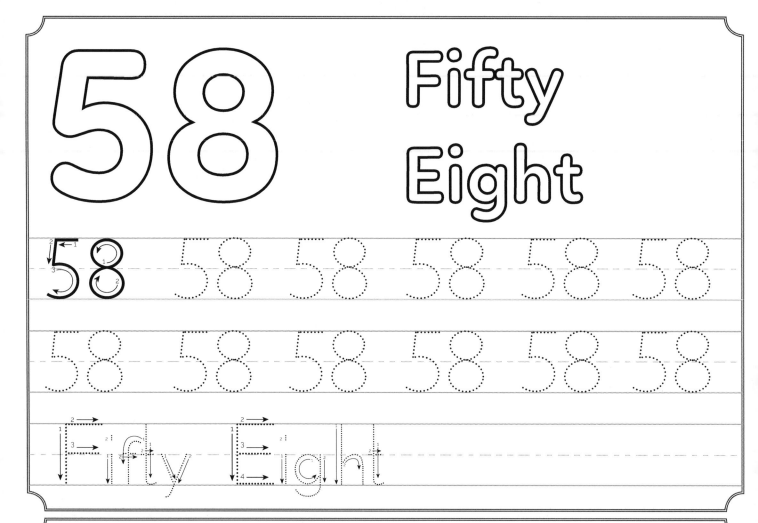

Write the time given on the clock.

59 Fifty Nine

Possum can not find eggs. Will you show him the way?

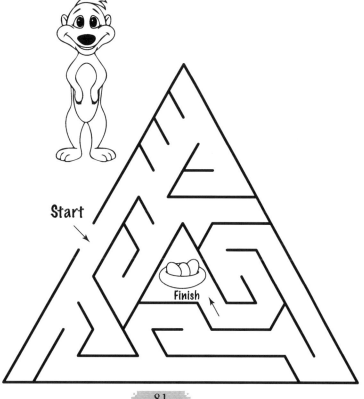

Start

Finish

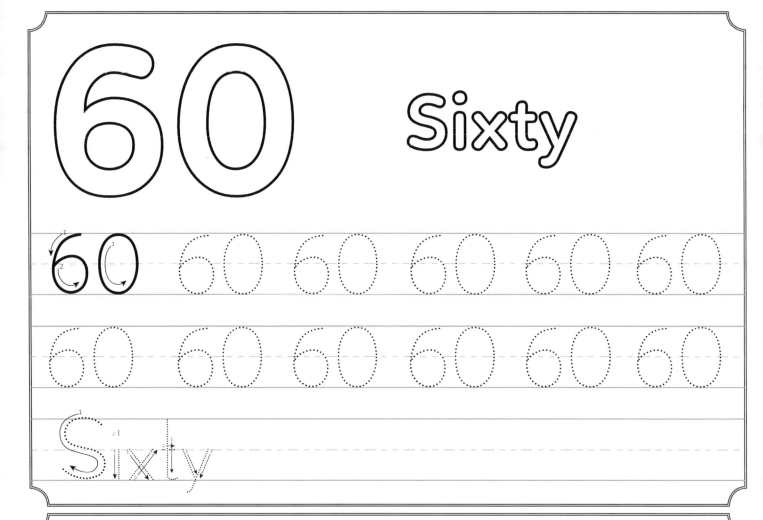

60 Sixty

60 60 60 60 60 60 60 60

60 60 60 60 60 60 60

Sixty

Choose the correct option to complete the cat.

A

B

C

D

61 Sixty One

Connect the dots and color it.

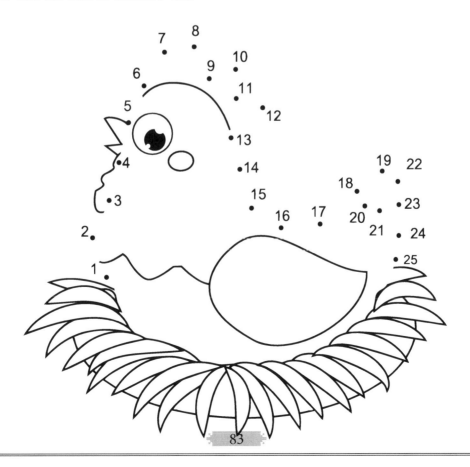

62

Sixty Two

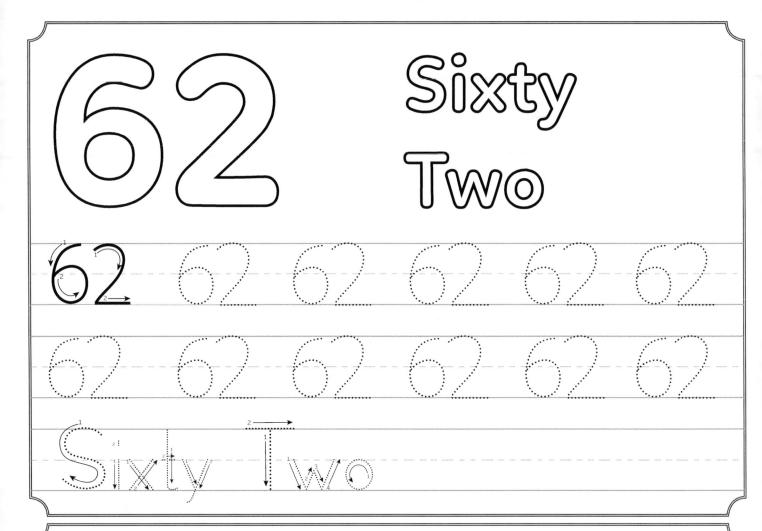

62 62 62 62 62 62 62
62 62 62 62 62 62 62

Sixty Two

Help the cat to find his food.

Start

Finish

63

Sixty Three

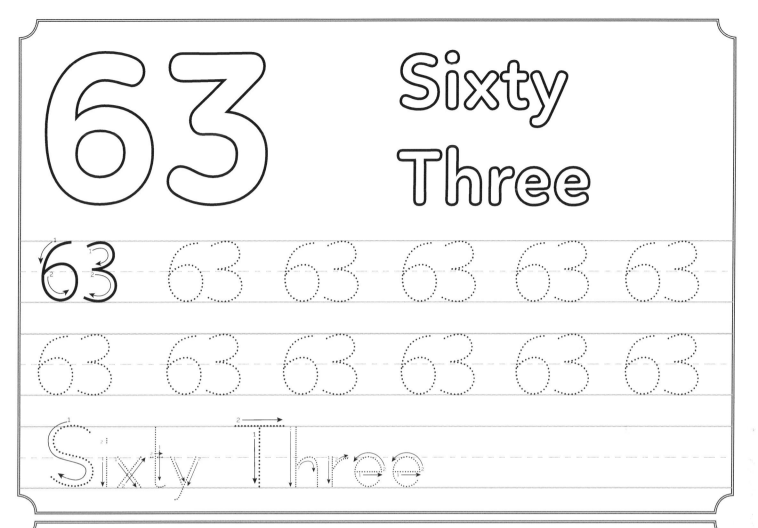

Draw a circle around each letter in the "sun".

64

Sixty Four

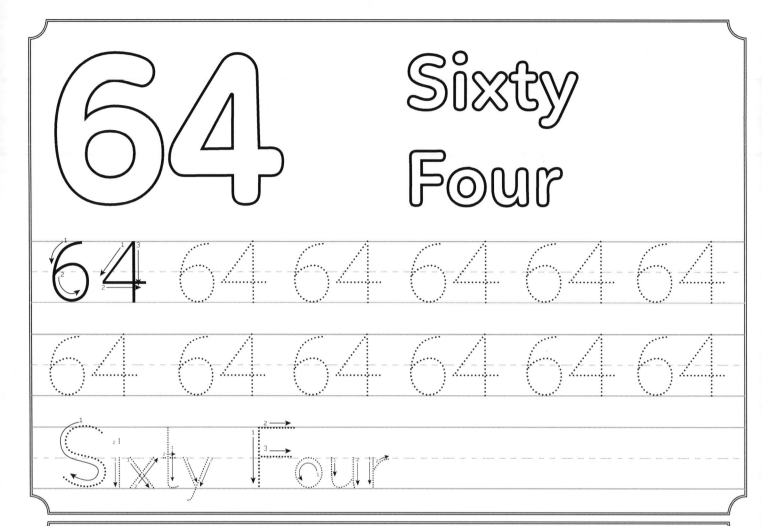

64 64 64 64 64 64

64 64 64 64 64 64 64

Sixty Four

Connect the dots and color it.

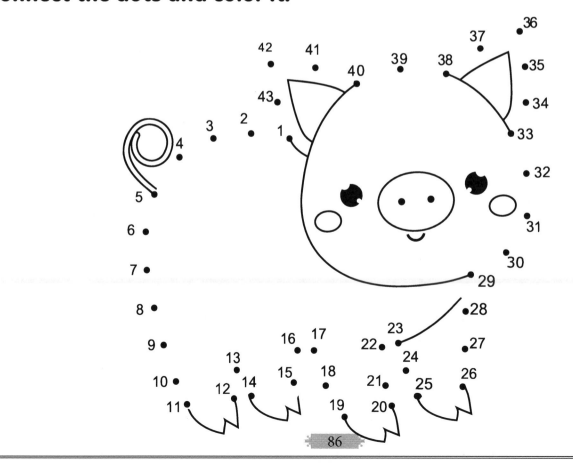

65 Sixty Five

65 65 65 65 65 65 65

65 65 65 65 65 65

Sixty Five

Choose the correct option to complete the pigeon.

A

B

C

D

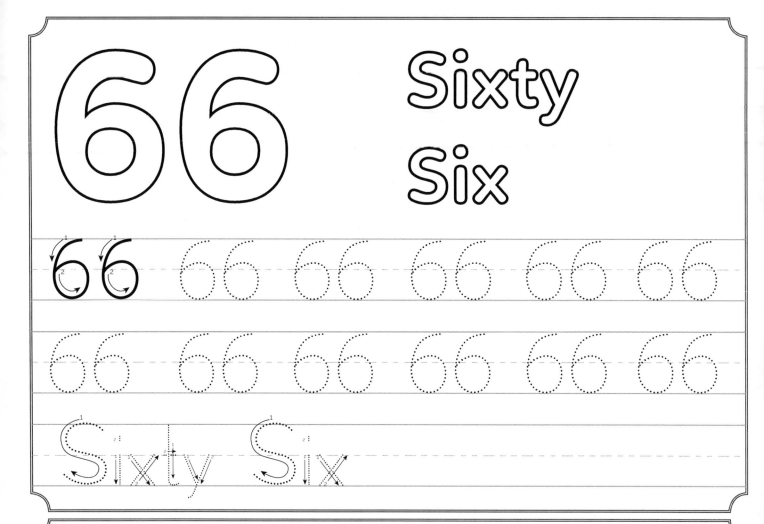

66 Sixty Six

66 66 66 66 66 66

66 66 66 66 66 66

Sixty Six

The bug can not find his leaf. Will you show him the way?

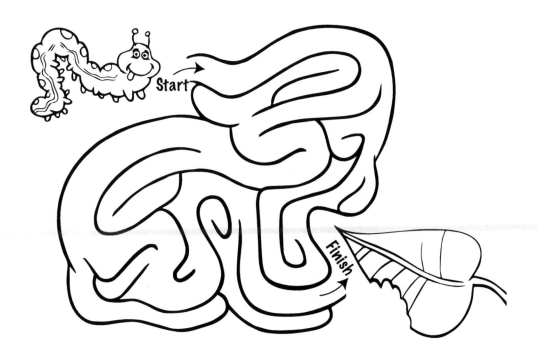

Start

Finish

67

Sixty Seven

67 67 67 67 67 67 67 67 67

67 67 67 67 67 67 67 67 67

Sixty Seven

Draw a circle around each letter in the "leaf".

68

Sixty Eight

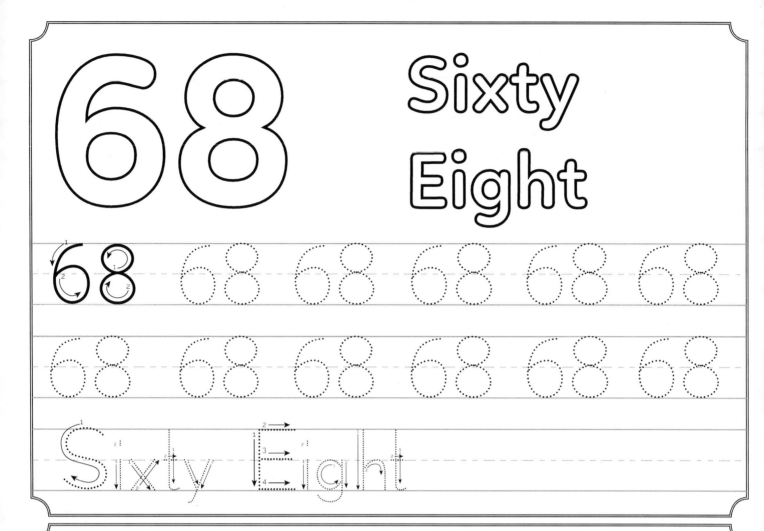

68 68 68 68 68 68 68 68 68

68 68 68 68 68 68 68 68 68 68

Sixty Eight

Connect the dots and color it.

69

Sixty Nine

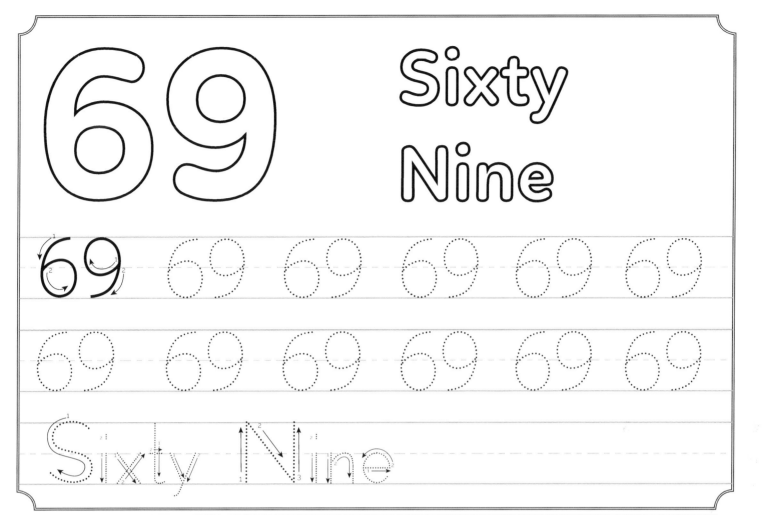

69   69   69   69   69   69

69   69   69   69   69   69

Sixty Nine

Write the time given on the clock.

70 Seventy

70 70 70 70 70 70

70 70 70 70 70 70

Seventy

Connect the dots and color it.

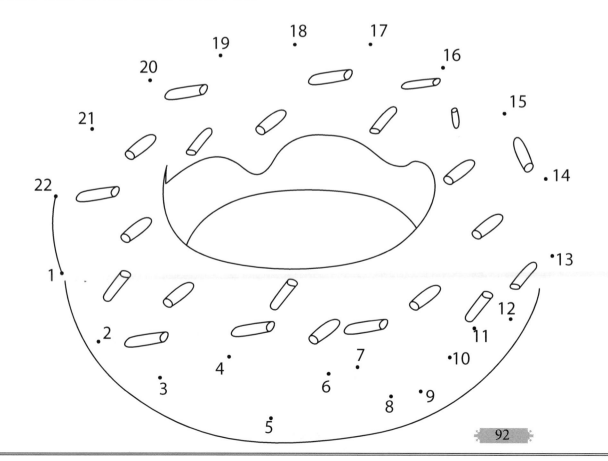

71

Seventy One

71 71 71 71 71 71 71 71 71 71 71 71

Seventy One

Snake can not find his food. Will you show him the way?

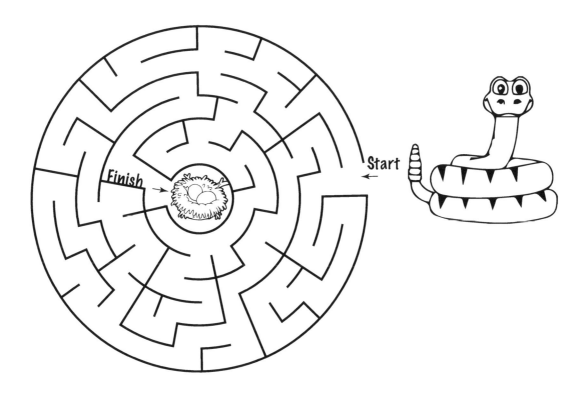

Finish   Start

72

Seventy Two

Choose the correct option to complete the fish.

A

B

C

D

73

Seventy Three

73 73 73 73 73 73 73

73 73 73 73 73 73 73

Seventy Three

Camel can not find his food. Will you show him the way?

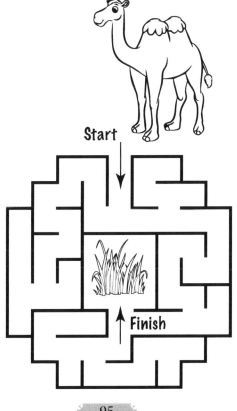

Start

Finish

74

Seventy Four

Connect the dots and color it.

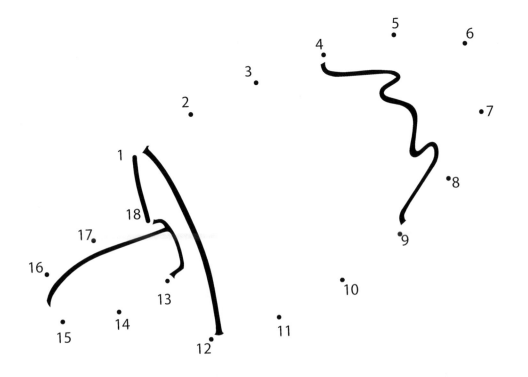

75

Seventy Five

75 75 75 75 75 75 75 75

75 75 75 75 75 75 75 75

Seventy Five

Write the time given on the clock.

76

Seventy Six

Draw a circle around each letter in the "cow".

77

Seventy Seven

77 77 77 77 77 77 77 77 77 77

77 77 77 77 77 77 77 77 77 77

Seventy Seven

Draw yours.

78

Seventy Eight

Connect the dots and color it.

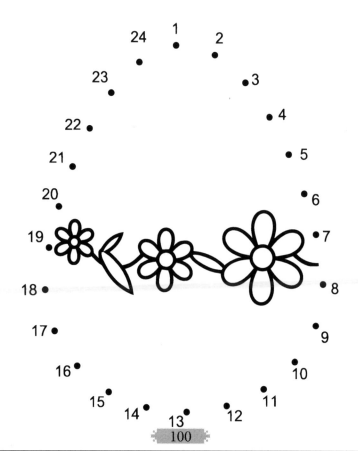

79

Seventy Nine

79 79 79 79 79 79 79

79 79 79 79 79 79 79

Seventy Nine

Choose the correct option to complete the vegetable.

A

B

C

D

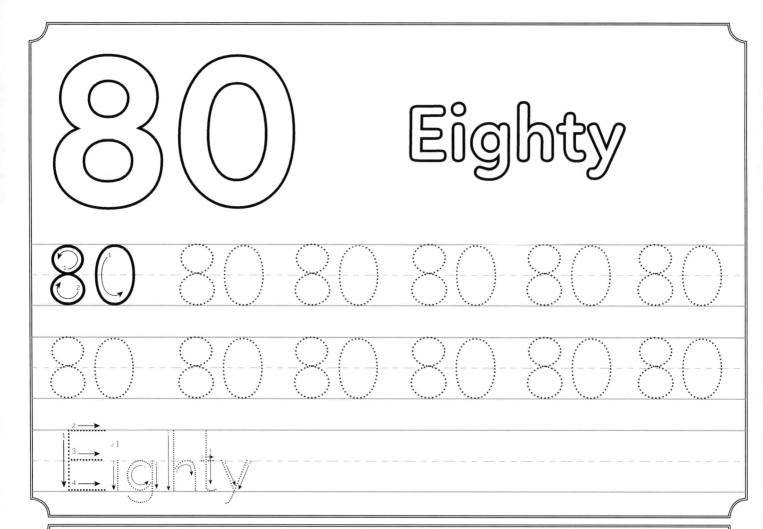

80

Eighty

80 80 80 80 80 80

80 80 80 80 80 80

Eighty

Hyena can not find the bird. Will you show him the way?

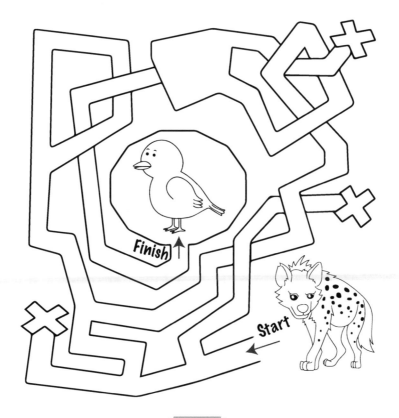

Finish

Start

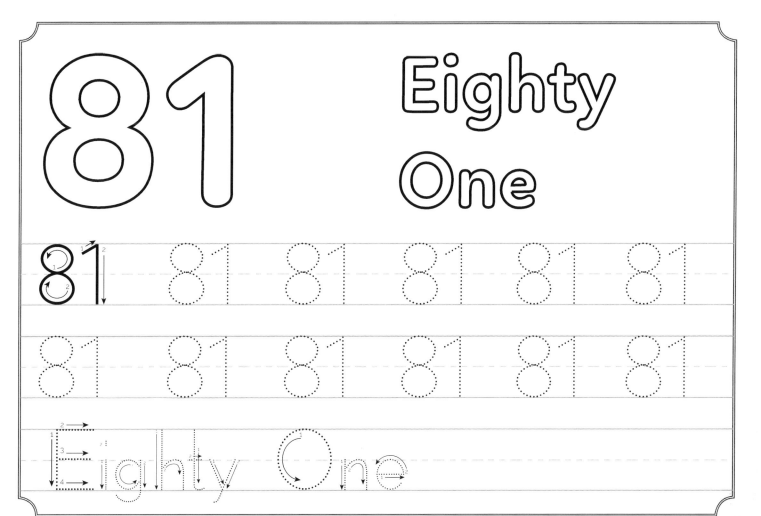

81

Eighty One

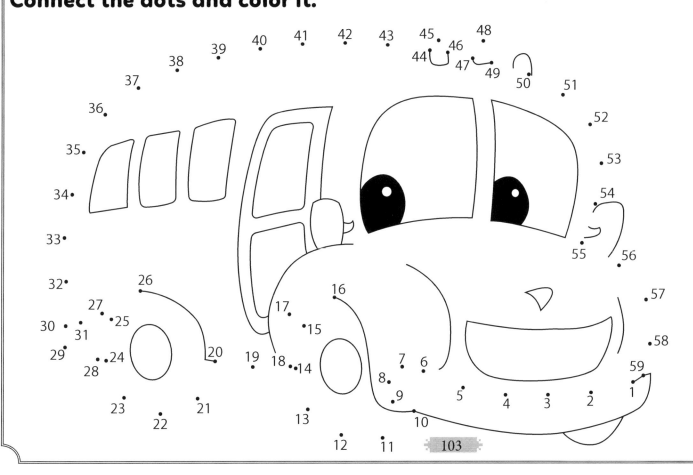

Connect the dots and color it.

82

Eighty Two

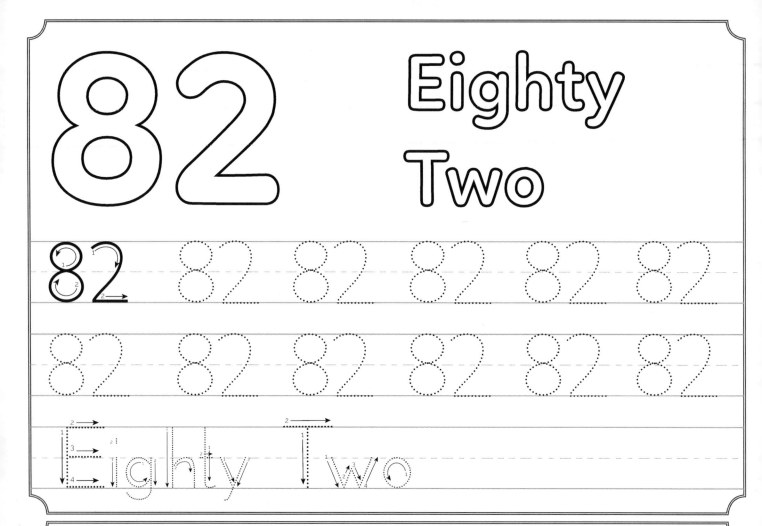

Draw a circle around each letter in the "DUCK".

83

Eighty Three

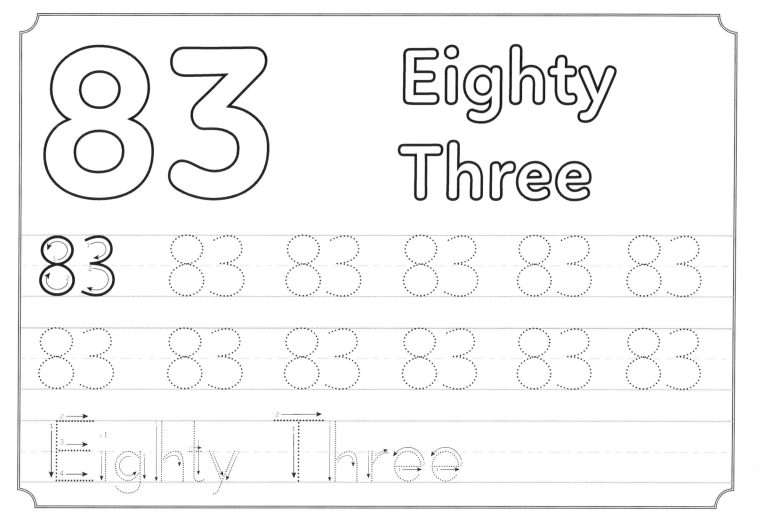

Choose the correct option to complete the picture.

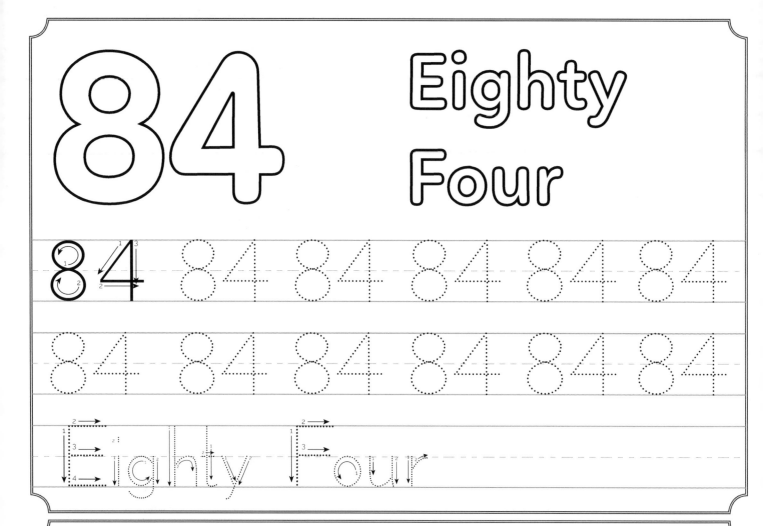

84

Eighty Four

Connect the dots and color it.

85

Eighty Five

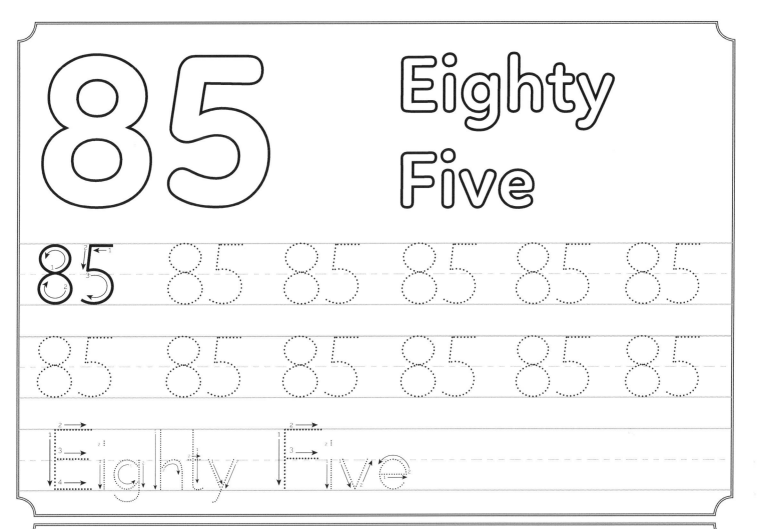

85 85 85 85 85 85

85 85 85 85 85 85

Eighty Five

The cat can not find the milk. Will you show him the way?

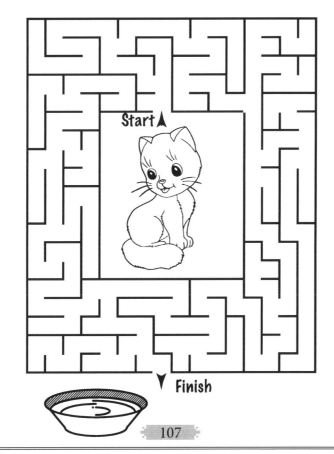

Start

Finish

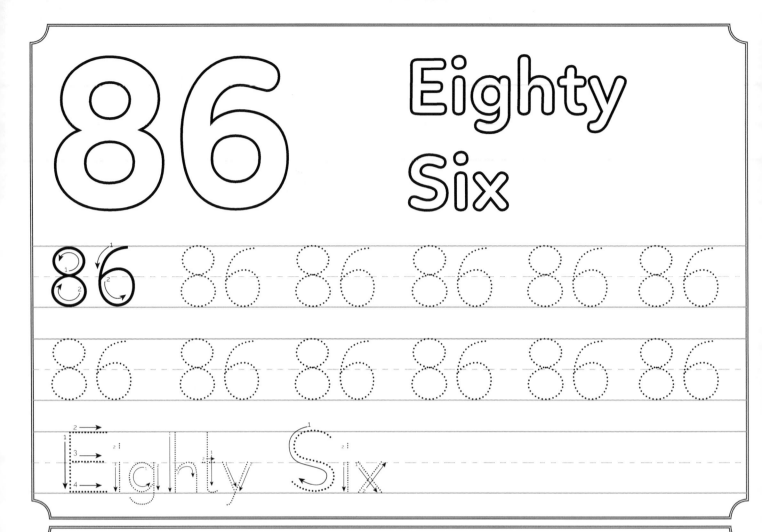

Connect the dots and color it.

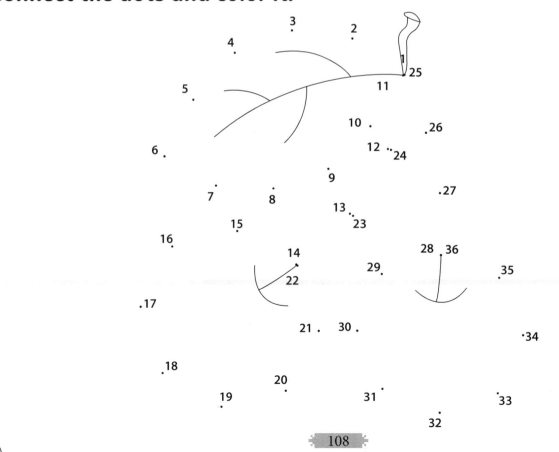

87

Eighty Seven

87 87 87 87 87 87 87

87 87 87 87 87 87

Eighty Seven

Choose the correct option to complete the deer.

A

B

C

D

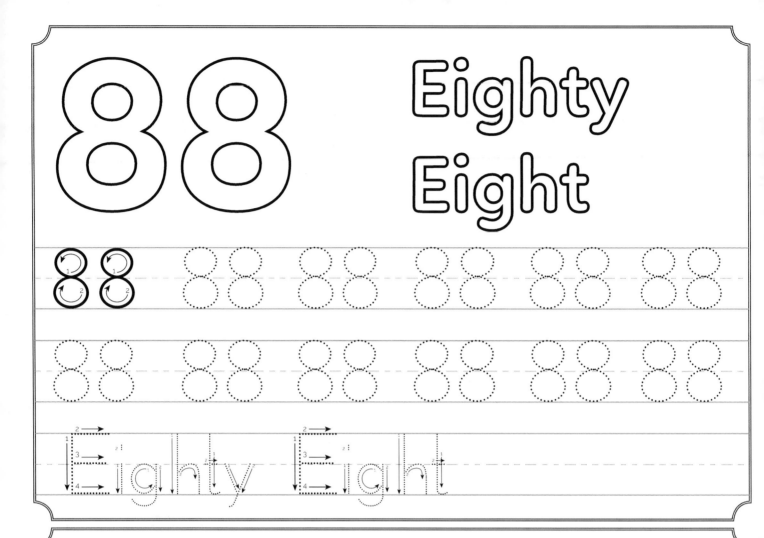

88

Eighty Eight

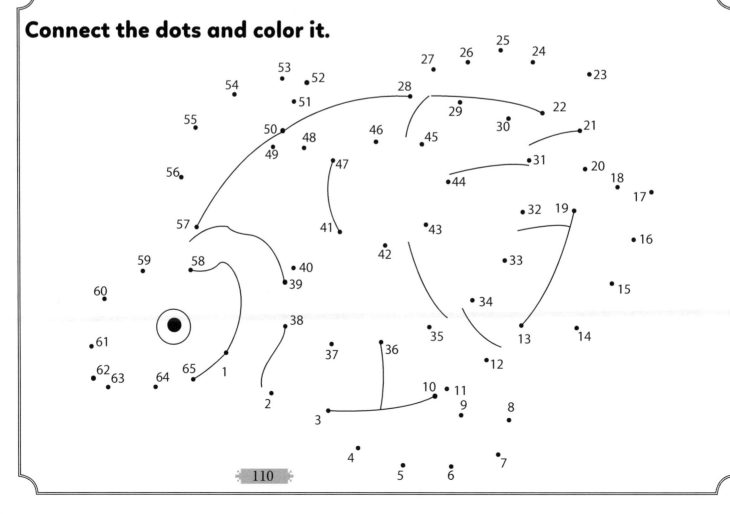

Connect the dots and color it.

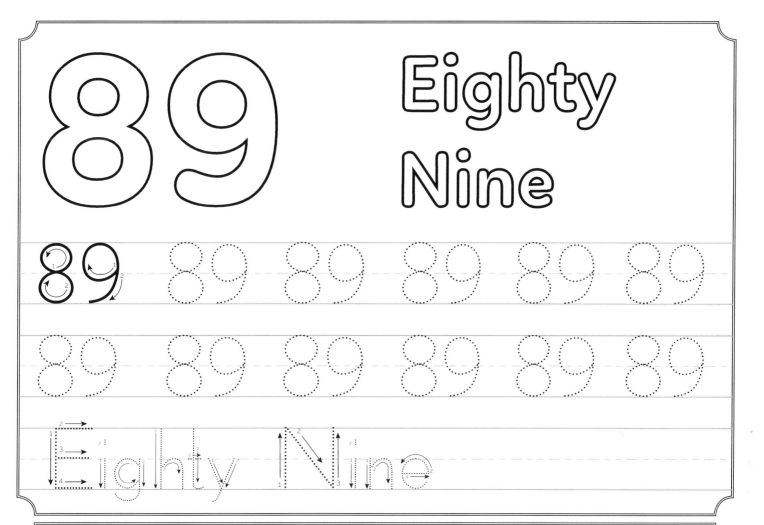

89

Eighty Nine

Connect the dots and color it.

90 Ninety

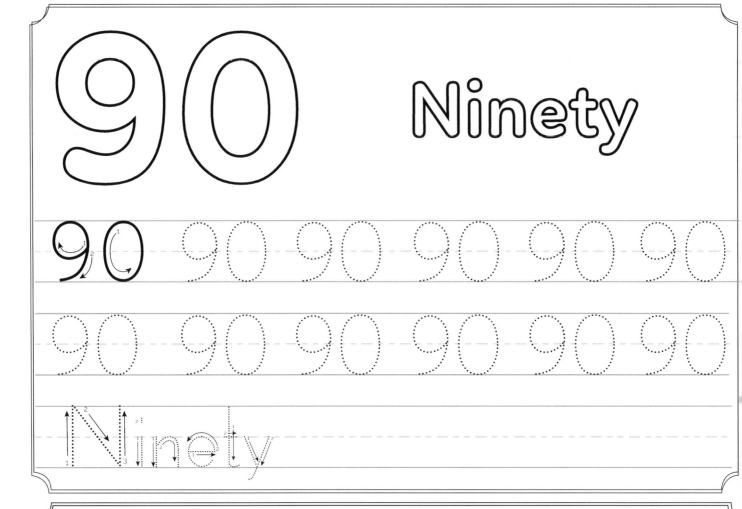

90 90 90 90 90 90 90
90 90 90 90 90 90 90

Ninety

Choose the correct option to complete the penguin.

A

B

C

D

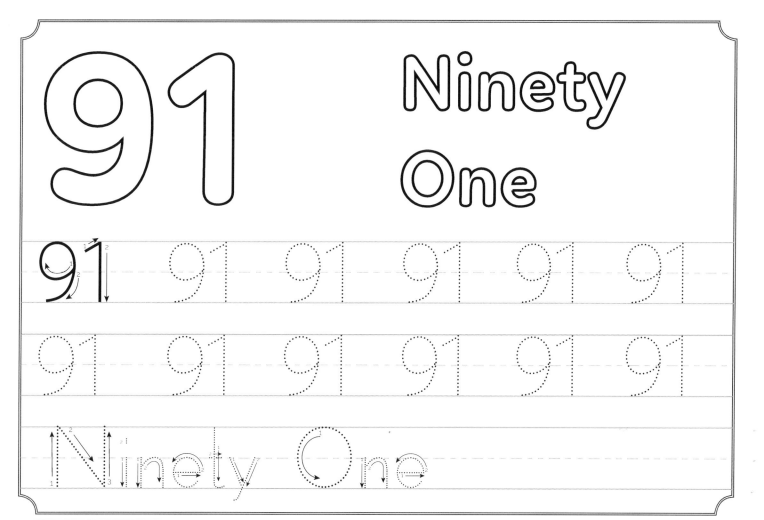

91 Ninety One

Connect the dots and color it.

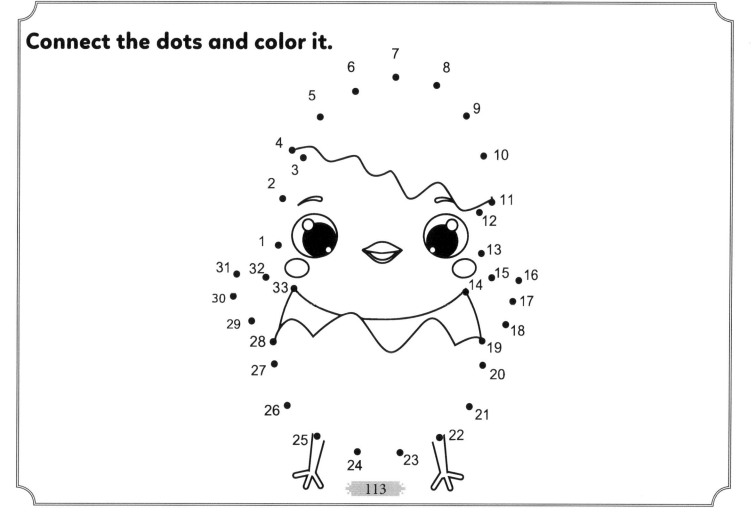

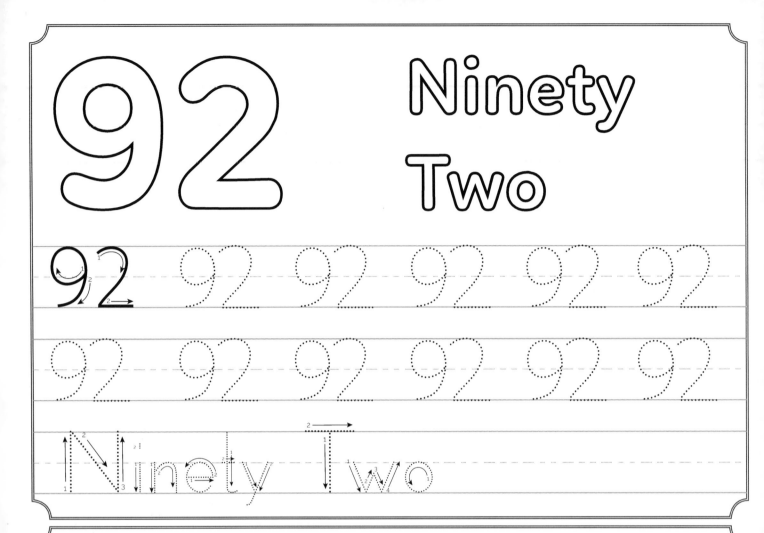

92

Ninety Two

92 92 92 92 92 92 92

92 92 92 92 92 92 92

Ninety Two

Write the time given on the clock.

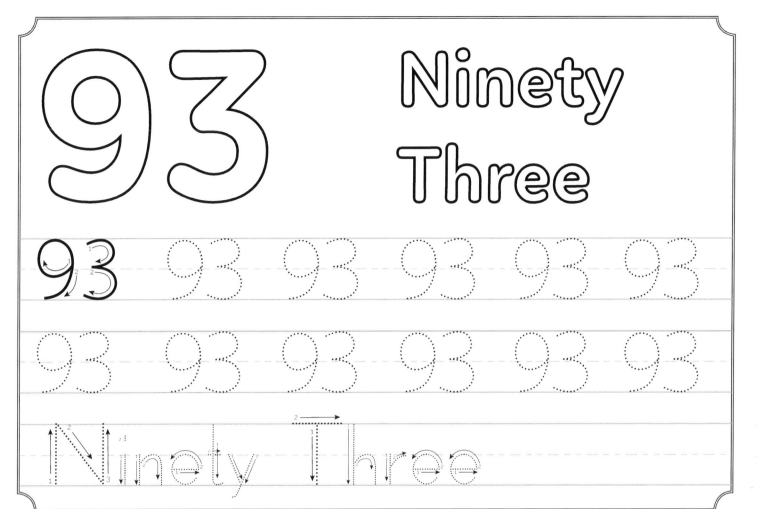

93

Ninety Three

93 93 93 93 93 93

93 93 93 93 93 93

Ninety Three

Bee can not find Flowers. Will you show him the way?

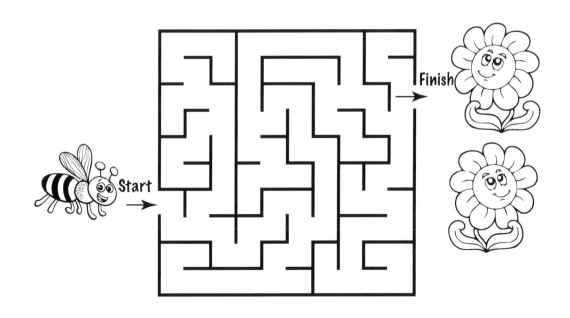

Start

Finish

94

Ninety Four

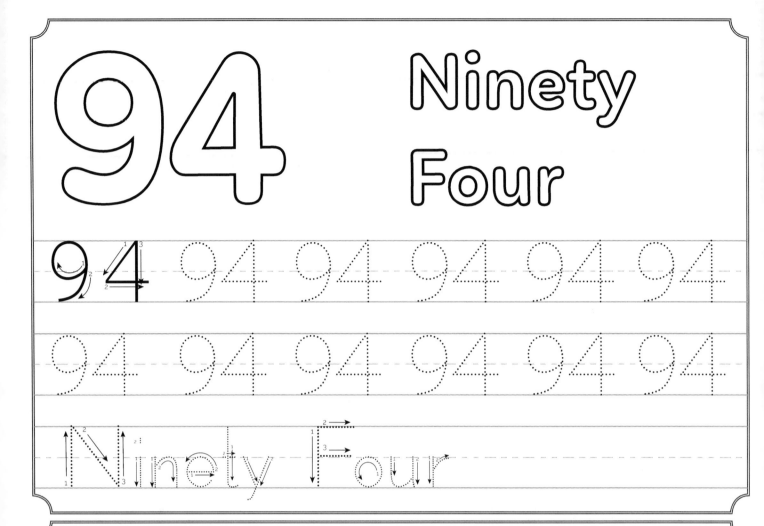

94 94 94 94 94 94
94 94 94 94 94 94

Ninety Four

The mouse can not find the cob. Will you show him the way?

Start

Finish

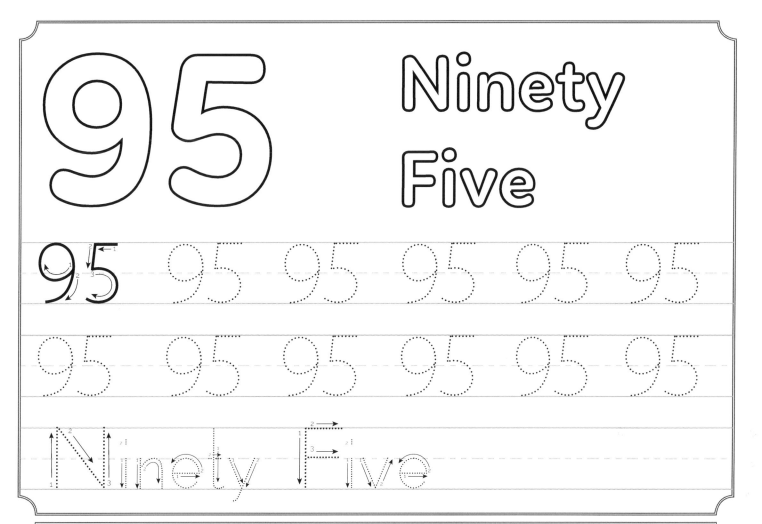

95

Ninety Five

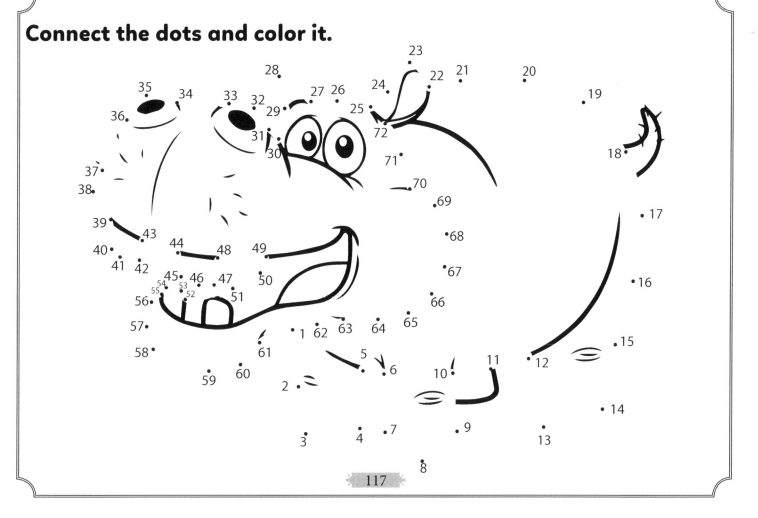

Connect the dots and color it.

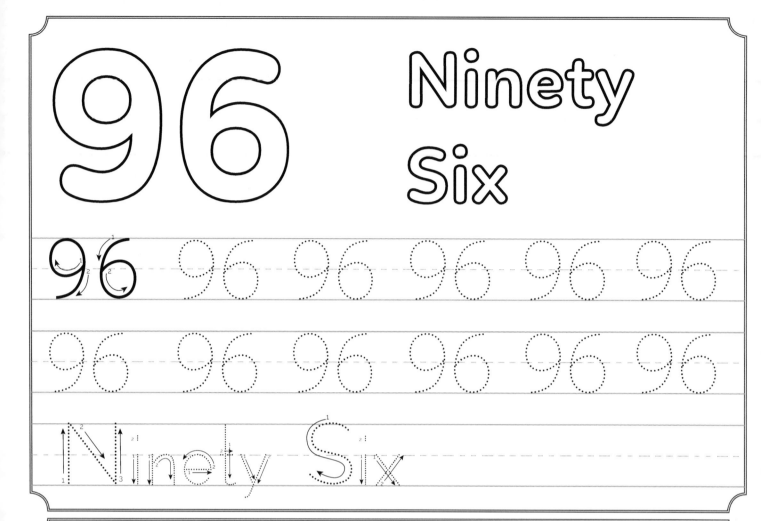

96 Ninety Six

Match the numbers with right words.

7

8

3

4

Four

Three

Eight

Seven

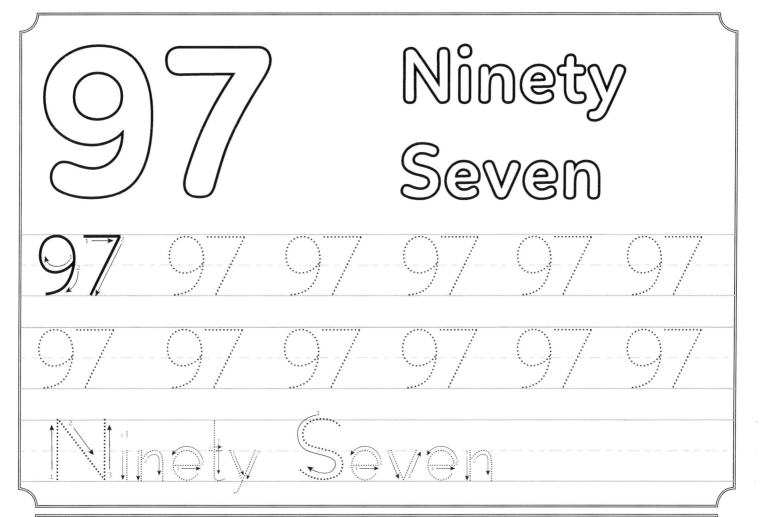

97
Ninety Seven

Connect the right option.

5

1

2

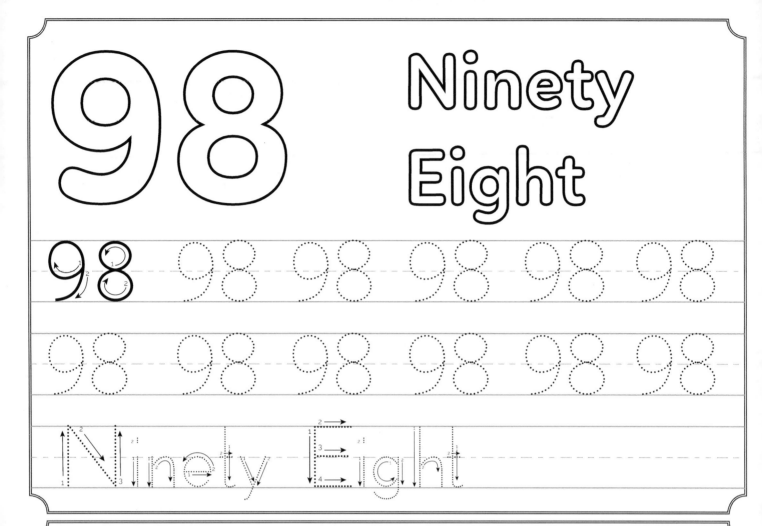

98 Ninety Eight

Connect the dots and color it.

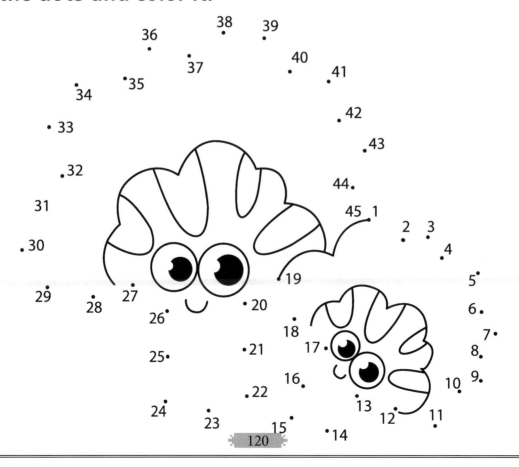

36 38 39
37 40
35 41
34 42
33 43
32 44
31 45 1
30 2 3
4
29 27 19 5
28 20 6
26 18 7
25 21 17 8
16 10 9
22 13 12 11
24 23 15 14

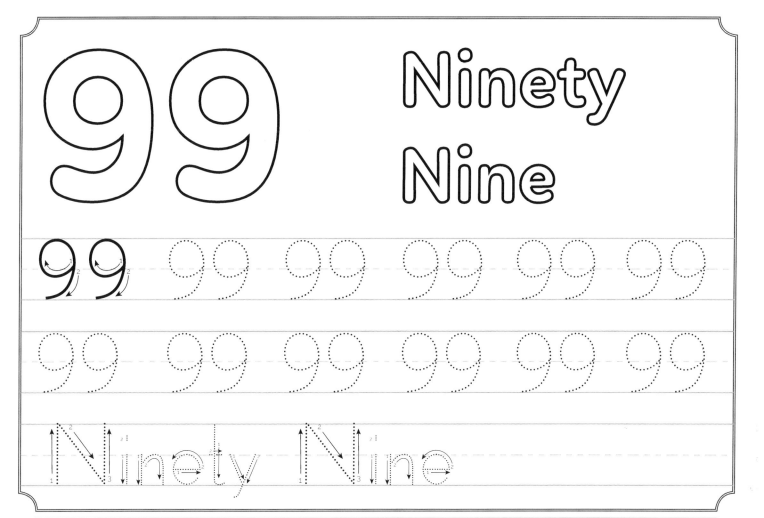

99 Ninety Nine

Complete the given number line and fill in the blanks.

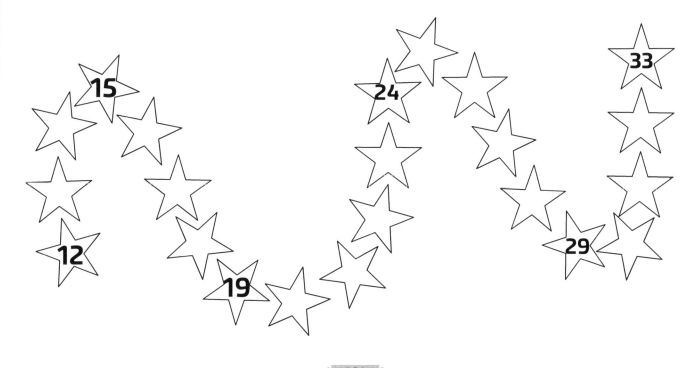

15

33

24

12

29

19

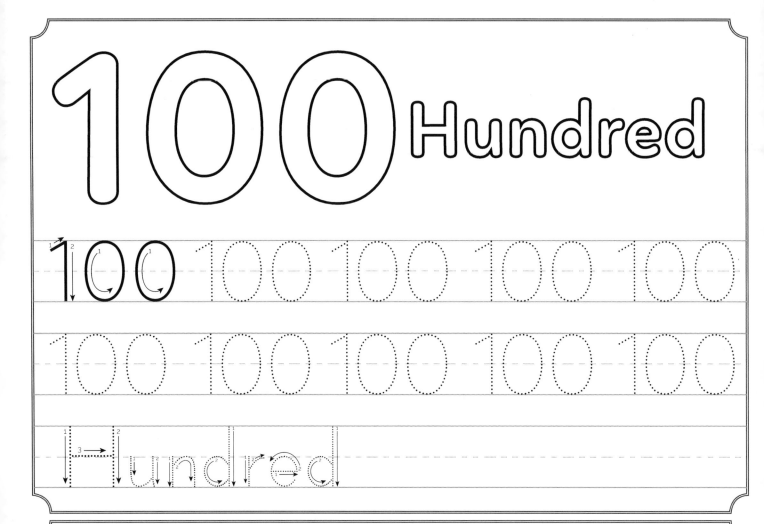

Complete the given number line and fill in the blanks.

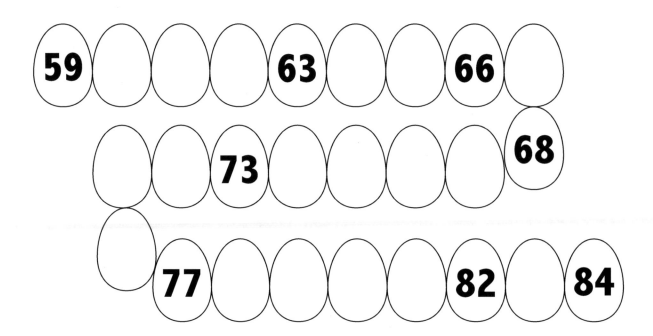

Would you like to receive periodically educational books and free teaching material to entertain your child?

Then sign up for the FB group of which I am co-administrator called
HAPPY LION CHILDREN'S BOOKS

https://www.facebook.com/groups/2882387582048536/

I wait for you

Happy Lion

Made in the USA
Columbia, SC
23 November 2021

49433869R00067